A HAND-BOOK FOR VISITORS TO LUCKNOW

A HAND-BOOK FOR VISITORS TO LUCKNOW

WITH PRELIMINARY NOTES
ON
ALLAHABAD AND CAWNPORE

H. G. KEENE

GYAN

Published by

Gyan Publishing House
5, Ansari Road
Daryaganj, New Delhi-110002
Phone: 011-47034999, 9811692060
E-mail: books@gyanbooks.com

Distribution Network
gyanbooks.com
India, USA, Canada, UK, Australia, France

ISBN : 978-81-212-3459-7 (PB)
First Published, Calcutta, 1875

2nd Impression 2020

Printed at: Gyan Press, Delhi.

A
Hand-Book for Visitors to Lucknow
Author: H. G. Keene

A

HAND-BOOK FOR VISITORS

TO

LUCKNOW

WITH PRELIMINARY NOTES ON ALLAHABAD AND CAWNPORE.

BY

H. G. KEENE,

AUTHOR OF "THE MOGUL EMPIRE FROM THE DEATH OF AURUNGZEB," &c.

CALCUTTA:

THACKER, SPINK AND CO.

BOMBAY: THACKER, VINING & Co. LONDON: W. THACKER & Co.

1875.

PREFACE.

THE following pages are mainly meant as an aid to the traveller visiting Lucknow. But he will, in all probability, pass through Allahabad and Cawnpore on his way; and both those places contain matter of interest, though not enough for an independent handbook.

Thanks are due to J. H. Prinsep, Esq., District Judge, C. McMinn, Esq., C. S., J. Bennett, Esq., Executive Engineer, T. Allan Browne, Esq., and other friends.

The Government system of transliteration has been generally adopted. The vowels *a*, *i*, and *u* are pronounced as in the English word "ruminant," except when accented, when the sound is broader. The other vowels as in "obey."

CONTENTS.

—:o:—

ALLAHABAD.

NOTES ON ALLAHABAD.

——:o:——

The provincial capital of the North-West Provinces does not contain objects of interest sufficient to furnish forth a regular Guide-book, or to detain the visitor more than a day or two. But at the same time there is enough to make it desirable that something should be recorded to enable the traveller to observe certain materials of information that are not to be found elsewhere.

The town is situated on the south-eastern extremity of the Döab, or "land of two rivers," on a tongue of land formed by the confluence of the Ganges, a river that drains the Eastern Himalayas, and the Jumna, whose affluents are derived from the western part of the same range, reinforced by the drainage of the Mewat Highlands, and the great chain of the Aravallis. The streams at the junction are nearly equal in volume; the Ganges, being the deeper, is of a yellow tint, and reputed more wholesome than the brighter and more attractive water of its shallower and swifter neighbour. The natives call the confluence *Tir Beni*, alleging that there is a third river—the Sarsuti or Saraswati—the lost river of the Sirhind plain, which flows underground to Allahabad; and, after irrigating the sacred tree of the catacomb in the Fort, issues out from beneath the walls, and joins its more ostentatious sisters.

The East Indian Railway crosses the Jumna just above the junction by a noble girder-bridge, which is also provided with a roadway for carriages and foot traffic, and is justly considered one of the wonders of Indian engineering.

The present city lies still further up the Jumna, and is a place of growing importance. In Heber's time, about half a century ago, it was "small, with very poor houses and small irregular streets." Fronting the glacis of the Fort, on the side of the city, was a *Jama Masjid*, or Cathedral Mosque, built by Shaista Khan, a celebrated general of Sháh Jahán's time; a large but unornamented place of worship, which, after having been repeatedly and most discreditably desecrated by the British residents, was ultimately removed in 1857, for strategic reasons, without any compensation, either in land or money, being bestowed on the Moslem community. The city meanwhile has been greatly improved under the municipal system of administration introduced within the last few years. It now contains 1,25,177 inhabitants, and can boast of a few fine new streets, and a covered market-place equal to that of a considerable county town in England. There is also a handsome Dispensary, dedicated to the memory of the late Hon'ble John Russell Colvin, and now about to be enlarged to the dimensions of a Hospital and Medical School.

Several large fairs are held on the river banks, which are a favourite place for those bathing pilgrimages which make Prayág (as the Hindus call it) rank with Benares, Hardwar, and Muttra as sacred scenes and resorts at certain appointed seasons.

Allahabad was once before the seat of the Local British Government, when things were done on a small and somewhat provisional scale. But it was never thought much of by the natives otherwise than in connection with the above-mentioned pilgrimages; and the superior advantages of Agra and its central situation led to the substitution of that city as the provincial metropolis. Soon after the mutiny the seat of Government was retransferred, Allahabad being considered more easily defensible.

In the last century it formed the seat of a subah or satrapy of the Empire. After the battle of Buxar it was assigned as a residence to the fugitive Prince Sháh Álum, who left it in 1771 in his ill-fated attempt to restore the greatness of his fathers by residing at Delhi. Allahabad was then occupied by the British, under whom it has continued ever since. It was described by an English traveller in 1782 as a miserable collection of thatched huts, and was then known to the Mahomedans by the derisive name of Fakirabad.

It is about 340 feet above the level of the sea, 496 miles from Calcutta, and 75 from Benares. It is in long. 81°55′ and lat. 25°26′. Of its early history little is known, and of that little there is but little trace left in the Allahabad of to-day. Nevertheless, it may be well that the visitor should have the means of informing himself of whatever is worth knowing; and may not, on his return to Europe, have to be indebted to foreign books for knowledge that is always better acquired on the spot. That little, therefore, must now be told.

In the dim distance of the earliest Indian history traces of a city—or at least of a fort—at the junction of the Ganges and Jumna are to be observed. In the third volume of his spirited and interesting resumé of the old Indian records (*History of India, Hindŭ, Buddhist, and Brahmanical*), Mr. Talboys Wheeler thus refers to the place:—

"The one point of paramount importance in all Hindustan is Allahabad, the ancient Prayága. Here the Vedic Rishis, inspired alike by poetic fancy and religious fervour, would approach the union of the two river deities with reverential awe. Here the Aryan Kshatryas, with true military instinct, appear to have constructed a fortress, which secured all the conquests on the upper valleys of the Jumna and Ganges, and overawed all lower Bengal."

From Tod we learn that the traditions of Rájasthán point to Prayága as the most ancient city of the Rajputs. His words are: "The ancient annals of the Jesalmer family of the Yadu stock give the priority of foundation to Poorág . . . at the confluence of the Yamuna and Ganges. The Prasü were the descendants of Pooru of Poorág, visited by Megasthenes Ambassador of Seleneus." Tod wrote before the full dayspring of ethnologic science; and was by nature credulous and talkative. But he knew the Rajput records; and his book is truly, in his own modest words, "a copious collection of materials for the future historian." There is no reason to doubt that a city stood where the rivers meet, in the days of the Macedonian Empire. Coming down to more recent times, the historian first quoted shows us the feast held by Siláditya, in the eighth century of the Christian era, in presence of the Chinese Buddhist Hwen Thsang. This was in the decline of Buddhism, probably not very long before the destruction of Sarnáth and the general rise of modern Hinduism. Nevertheless, Mr. Wheeler finds that from the days of the Vedic Aryans, down to this period, Prayága had never ceased to be the holiest spot in Hindustan, the "field of happiness," where it was as meritorious to bestow the smallest copper coin in alms as it would be to lavish a *lakh* elsewhere.

Turning from this literary evidence, which may be strong but cannot be considered abundant, we find ample confirmation of it in the two important relics remaining in the Fort—the obelisk, or *lath* of Asoka, and the very ancient subterranean temple containing the sacred tree. These, however, will hereafter be described at some length; and the attention of the visitor is only drawn to them here in passing.

THE STATION, CIVIL AND MILITARY.

The visitor at Allahabad from Bombay or Calcutta is landed at the Railway-station of the East Indian Railway, one of the first that was finished and opened for traffic after the suppression of the disturbances that followed on the mutiny of the Bengal Army in 1857. The bridge by which he has just crossed the broad Jumna is thrown over that river just above its confluence with the Ganges, and has already been noticed as one of the greatest exploits of modern engineering in India, being of the extraordinary length of 3,331 lineal feet. To the south he has now the city and the Khushru Bagh; to the east the old Moghul Fort; to the west the "Grand Trunk Road," leading to Cawnpore, and away to the far north-west; to the north the British Cantonments, the new settlement of Cannington, and the old civil lines, in one or other of which localities he will probably find his friends; or, if he be not provided with letters of introduction, a choice of good hotels.

The Station—as Anglo-Indian custom denominates the "White-town" of Allahabad—consists of two parts. To the immediate front of the railway lies the new settlement of Cannington, designed by the late Mr. C. B. Thornhill, since Allahabad was fixed on as the site of the capital for the North-West Provinces transferred from Agra after the mutinies. It contains a number of wide streets, or "roads," as they are locally called, laid out in building-sites, now mostly occupied with houses, and crossing each other at right angles like those of a modern city in the United States. These roads are all well-planted with teak and other timber trees, and each bears the name of some person of local or imperial celebrity. Thus, parallel with the "City Road," run the "Queen's Road" and "Albert Road," while transversely run "Canning" and "Elgin" Roads. The longest road of all, joining the extreme west side towards the Railway with the extreme east or old station backed by the Ganges, is appropriately named after Mr. Thornhill. Emerging from the Railway-station, the traveller comes upon the nascent Anglican Church, still (1875) in a very backward condition.

Further on is the large pile of buildings erected for the Government Press; and then come the "palatial" barracks of the British Infantry. These well-meant structures, for which India is indebted to Lord Sandhurst, most unfortunately situated in a low, unhealthy, and in every respect ill-chosen locality, are on a bend of the Ganges. Turning to the right up the Thornhill Road, we come upon the N. W. P. Club, the Roman Catholic Orphanage, and the Alfred Park, another unhappily selected site. Here will be found a memorial hall, dedicated to the memory of Mr. Thornhill, and another distinguished Civil Officer, the late Mr. F. O. Mayne, C.B., a piece of pretentious architecture intended to contain a Library and Museum. On the opposite side of the road, a large and handsome pile of adapted Saracenic architecture is being raised for the use of the new Central College, to be known by the name of an Ex-Lieutenant-Governor Sir William Muir. Still further on is the Government House, a plain but very well situated building, consisting of a central set of public rooms flanked by curved wings, and standing on a rising ground surrounded by a very pretty garden. To the right or south of this are the meadow lands leading down to the glaçis of the Fort and the "meeting of the waters." These meadows were originally intended for the People's Park; and it is to be hoped that they may yet be utilised some day for the purpose, abounding as they do in wood and water, and having natural advantages which the Alfred Park can never realise.

On the other side, to the north of the College, lies the old station, of which nothing need be said, excepting that it contains an old fashioned church in the most hideous style of the late unlamented "Military-Board," built in 1839; and a number of very comfortable bungalows and barracks of the old fashioned type, built when coolness was more thought of than outward display. Here, on the 5th of June 1857, took place the mutiny of the 6th Bengal Native Infantry. The officers, on hearing the disturbance caused by the mutineers adjoining, ran from their mess-house to the parade-ground, where they were all destroyed with the exception of nine unposted Ensigns, who were bayonetted in the house. The treasury was then looted, the district-jail broken loose, the bungalows burned, and some 50 of the general white population massacred. The rest of the non-combatants took refuge in the Fort, where they were protected by the gallant Brasyer, at the head of 400 Sikhs and a few European gunners; and on the 11th they were relieved by the famous Colonel Neill at the head of a detachment of his regiment (now the 102nd Fusiliers).

THE KHUSHRU BAGH.

On the city side of the Railway-station, and almost immediately facing the entrance, is an old archway overgrown with creepers, by which admission is obtained to an extensive and well-kept garden. This was probably once the pleasure-ground of Salim, the son of the Great Emperor Akbar, afterwards himself Emperor with the title of Jahángir. This Prince, during the latter years of his father's reign, was Governor of the Fort of Allahabad and its dependent provinces, and resided in the palace with his wives, one of whom was a Hindu Princess of the house of Marwar or Jodhpur, and another a daughter of the Raja of Amber, now Jaipur. The former bore Khurram, afterwards the Emperor Sháh Jahán; but the son of the latter was his elder brother. On this prince—born in 995 A. H. (corresponding to A. D. 1588)—had been bestowed the name of Khushru, or "Fairface," an old name of the Achœmenian kings of Persia, the "Cyaxares" of classical Greek, the "Ahasuerus" of Scripture. It may surprise some persons to find the name of this ancient Zoroastrian given to a Mahomedan prince; but it must never be forgotten that the Persians, from whom Akbar was partially descended, have never cordially embraced the religion of their Islamite conquerors. Some are nominally Musulmans, but only of the Shiah sect; and there are many forms of rank heresy among them. Another large portion left their native seats and became the founders of the flourishing Parsee community of the present day. Sufceism, Babism, Atheism itself (as in the case of the Astronomer-Poet Omar Khayyam) long sustained the national spirit in estrangement from the Arab invaders; and when Akbar became Emperor of India, one of his main ambitions was to diminish the influence of the Mahomedan Church, and restore some at least of the tenets of fire-worship. It was probably as a part of this policy that he selected for his grandsons such names as Khushru, a system of nomenclature which afterwards became hereditary among his descendants.

The mother of Khushru was the daughter of Raja Bhagwan Das, head of the Kachwaha Rajputs, and sister, by adoption, of her first cousin, the celebrated Rája Mán Singh. Her husband, Prince Salim, had given much trouble to Akbar; and it was Mán Singh's hope to bring forward his own nephew (the prince's eldest son) to supplant the father as heir-apparent. Distracted by these intrigues, and probably despairing of seeing any reformation in the character of either her husband or her son, the mother of Khushru took an overdose of opium: but Salim succeeded in pacifying his father, and mounted the throne without a struggle. Khushru on this fled towards Lahore in the vain hope of raising the country in his own favour. These events occurred in A.D. 1605. Khushru was pursued, his party broken up, and its leaders put to painful and disgraceful deaths. Pardoned, but not trusted, Khushru was shortly after once again on rebellion. When next secured, he was made over for safe keeping to the person most interested in putting him out of the way—his younger brother Prince Khurram. This youth, then only 22 years of age, was just proceeding to assume the Government of the Deccan; and, in his charge, the unfortunate and ill-guided Khushru died; Mán Singh, his uncle (who had been his worst counsellor, but who was at the head of 20,000 devoted Rájput troops) escaping with a heavy fine.

Khushru appears to have been a favourite with the people; while his father and brother were probably not unwilling to do all that could be effected by a reasonable outlay of money to do honour to his memory, now that he could trouble them no more. They therefore declared him a martyr, and erected to his memory a handsome mausoleum in the garden close by where his mother had been buried in 1606.

Khushru died in 1615; but we learn from the inscription that his tomb was not finished till seven years later. It is a large and handsome domed building in the style of which Humaiun's tomb at Delhi, and the famous Taj, are the best known specimens. The true tomb, as usual in Moghul sepulchres, is under-ground; the building which contains the cenotaph is large and lofty; and the plaster of the interior has been painted with birds and flowers in a style which must once have been brilliant and is still full of spirit.

A little to the westward of the tomb of Khushru is another handsome tomb, much resembling that of Islam Khan at Fathipur-Sikri. The inscriptions are much defaced, but it is believed to be quite empty, having been built for Khushru's sister, who died and was buried elsewhere.

The next, a quaint, four-sided, two storied place, is supposed to be the tomb of the ill-fated Kachwaha lady, the mother of Khushru, and cousin of Mán Singh, called in the inscriptions "Sháh Begum." On the opposite side of the road, the house now occupied by the Superintendent of the Gardens, is traditionally known as the house of the "Tamboli Begum." This possibly may be the same that is, at Fathipur-Sikri, called the Lady of of Constantinople or "*Istamboli Begum.*"

The garden is kept up by the municipality, and is a favourite resort for the residents as a place for *fêtes* and open-air gatherings.

The following may be taken as a free version of the inscription on the grave of the Prince:—

Ah! woe, that in high Heaven's award Caprice should conquer Right,
'Twas even so that came the woe, when Justice took to flight;
When Life beyond the bounds of Bliss her canvass house unfurled,
Because Corruption sapped the deep foundations of the World.

The World has felt Heaven's terrors; for, wheree'r the flames have spread
The very ashes out of sight are altogether sped;
Autumn, he knew, is coming when the fullest bloom is seen,
Yet Wisdom he forewent to be the Bulbul of the green.

But what avails the verdure when the thorn of Death at last
Its hundred steel-points through the folds of silken robes has cast?
Or how should I the truth declare with lips that sighing burns,
While the Globe rolls her freight of souls the truth that still returns?
"The flower that sprang, the bird that sang, have perished on the thorns;
For whom the Earth laments below, the Sky above them mourns!"

And thus the robe of Majesty was turned to punishment,
When Sultan Khushru got the word to march and strike his tent;
And that fair body which had scarcely brooked the garb of mirth,
Woe's me! was fain to bear as best it might the load of earth.

Then follows the usual stanza, stating how the Poet was inspired to find the Chronogram "(His mighty soul fills a Court of Paradise)"—A. H. 1031, A.D. 1623.

THE FORT.

It has been already mentioned that the Fort of Allahabad stands exactly at the confluence of the Ganges and Jumna. The, existing castle was built by the Great Emperor Akbar about the year 1575 A.D. But from the presence of the Buddhist remains already referred to, it may be inferred that the site was the centre of the old Hindu city said to be the oldest Capital of the Lunar or *Somabansi* dynasty of Kshattris (Growse's *Mathura*, p. 81).

Heber noticed how much the picturesque character of a mediæval castle had been sacrificed to the improvements dictated by the military science of his day; and the process has gone on since: the "lofty towers being pruned down, and the high stone ramparts topped with turf parapets, and obscured by a green sloping glaçis." The worst part of the business, however, is not this so much as the wanton facing of the massive and yet graceful Moghul structures with hideous plaster masonry, in which the Greek Order is introduced in the most uncompromising style of the late ill-famed Military Board. It, the M. B., has fastened with peculiar gusto on the entrance. This gateway in Heber's time was surmounted by a dome with a wide hall beneath, surrounded by arcades and galleries, and ornamented with rude but glowing paintings, so as to form the noblest approach to a place of arms that the accomplished Prelate had ever seen. It will now, with some careful search, be detected as the nucleus of the "Wellesley ravelin." The rest of the palace exists in the same eclipsed condition, but so disguised as to be hardly worth visiting.

But in the wide space between the above-mentioned entrance and the gate of the Arsenal will be seen on object of real importance in excellent preservation,—namely the lofty and elegant monolith of Asoka. The most accurate and instructive description of this monument will be found in the first volume of Cunningham's *Archæological Reports.*

"As the old city of *Praydg* has totally disappeared, we can scarcely expect to find any traces of the various Buddhist monuments which were seen and described by the Chinese pilgrim in the 7th century. Indeed, from their position to the south-west of the city, it seems very probable that they may have been washed away by the Jumna even before the final abandonment of the city, as the course of that river for three miles above the confluence has been due west and east of many centuries past. At any rate, it is quite certain that no remains of these buildings are now to be seen; the only existing Hindu monument being the well-known stone pillar which bears the inscriptions of Asoka Samudra Gupta, and Jahângir. As Hwen Thsang makes no mention of this pillar, it is probable that it was not standing in his day. Even its original position is not exactly known, but it was probably not far from its present site. It was first erected by King Asoka about B.C. 240 for the purpose of inscribing his edicts regarding the propagation of Buddhism. It was next made use of by Samudra Gupta, about the second century of the Christian era, for the reçord of his extensive sovereignty over the various nations of India—from Nepâl to the Dakhan, and from Gujarât to Assam. Lastly, it was re-erected by the Mogal Emperor Jahângir to commemorate his accession to the throne in the year 1605 A.D. These are the three principal inscriptions on the Allahabad Pillar, but there are also a number of minor records of the names of travellers and pilgrims of various dates, from about the beginning of the Christian era down to the present century. Regarding these minor inscriptions, James Prinsep remarks that 'it is a singular fact that the periods at which the pillar has been overthrown can be thus determined with nearly as much certainty from this desultory writing, as can the epochs of its being re-erected from the more formal inscriptions recording the latter event. Thus that it was overthrown some time after its first erection by the great Asoka in the middle of the third century before Christ, is proved by the longitudinal or random insertion of several names in a character intermediate between No. 1 and No. 2, in which the *m*, *b*, &c., retain the old form. Of one of these names he remarks.—' Now it would have been exceedingly difficult, if not impossible, to have cut the name No. 10 up and down at right angles to the other writing, *while the pillar was erect*, to say nothing of the place being out of reach, unless a scaffold were erected on purpose, which would hardly be the case, since the object of an ambitious visitor would be defeated by placing his name out of sight and in an unreadable position.' The Pillar 'was erected as Samudra Gupta's arm,' and there it probably remained until overthrown again by the idol-breaking zeal of the Musulmâns; for we find no writings on it of the *Pâla*, or Sârnâth type (*i.e.*, of the tenth century), but a quantity appears with plain legible dates from the *Samvat* year 1420, or A. D. 1363, down to 1660 odd, and it is remarkable that these occupy one side of the shaft, or that which was uppermost when the pillar was in a prostrate position. A few detached and ill-executed Nâgari names with *Samvat* dates of 1800 odd, 'show that ever since it was laid on the ground again by General Garstin, the passion for recording visits of piety or curiosity has been at work.'* In this last passage James Prinsep has, I believe, made a mistake in the name of the Vandal Engineer who overthrew the stone pillar because it stood in the way of his new line of rampart near the gateway. It was General Kyd, and not General Garstin, who was employed to stengthen the Fort of Allahabad, and his name is still preserved in the suburb of Kyd-ganj, on the Jumna, immediately below the city.

"The pillar was again set up in 1838 by Captan Edward Smith, of the Engineers, to whom the design of the present capital is entirely due. At first it was intended to have placed a fancy flower as an appropriate finish to the pillar, but as the people had a tradition that the column was originally surmounted by the figure of a lion, it was suggested by a committee of the Asiatic Society that the design of the new capital should be made as nearly as possible the same as the original, of which the Bakra and Lauriya pillars were cited as examples. The lion statues

---

* Bengal Asiatic Society's Journal, 1837, p. 967.

which crown the bell capitals of these two pillars I have seen and admired, and I can affirm that they are the figures of veritable lions. Both of them are represented half couchant, with the head raised and the mouth open. The bell capital swells out boldly towards the top to receive a massive abacus, which forms the plinth of the statue. In these examples the broad swelling capital is in harmony with the stout and massive column. But the new capital designed by Captain Smith is, in my opinion, a signal failure. The capital lessens towards the top, and is surmounted by an abacus of less diameter than that of the pillar itself. The animal on the top is small and recumbent, and altogether the design is insignificant. Indeed, it looks to me not unlike a stuffed poodle stuck on the top of an inverted flower pot."

The modern Hindu mythologists have appropriated this pillar, which goes by the name among them of "Bhim Sen's Club;" reminding one of the articles attributed in England to King Arthur or Guy, Earl of Warwick. The edicts of Asoka referred to by the General have been read here, and elsewhere; for they are found in various distant parts of India. They are of twofold character: one enlarging on the doctrine, occasionally occurring in the prophetical parts of the Hebrew Scriptures that the practice of virtue is the best sacrifice; and the other inculcating the sacredness of life and the sin of destroying or even of neglecting it in the case of animals as well as of men. By the mention of the son of Seleucus and of other successors of Alexander the Great, the date has been approximately fixed about the middle of the second century before the Christian era.

As to the erection by the Emperor Jahángir being the last, the General corrects himself further down. The pillar he tells us was once more erected in 1838 by Capt. E. Smith of the Bengal Engineers. It appears from Thornton's *Gazeteer* that this final elevation was thus brought about. When the Jesuit father Tiefenthaler visited Allahabad about the middle of last century, the pillar was still standing as the Moghul had reared it. But in 1798 some alterations being made in the Fort, this ancient and valuable relic was taken down; and was actually used as a roller for the parade-ground, when Lord Auckland once more restored its fallen greatness. Following, very properly, the examples of two not very distant pillars in the old kingdom of Magadha (of which drawings will be found at p. 59 of Cunningham's Volume above-cited) the Government ordered that the top of the column, which was unfinished, should be crowned with the figure of a lion seated upon an abacus of stone. Unfortunately the execution was not equal in merit to the conception. The height of the pillar as given in Thornton is 42 feet; and the form is cylindrical, but slightly tapering, the base diameter being three feet, two and a quarter inches, while that at the summit is no more than two feet two; being a slope of about one foot in forty.

In front of monuments of this class it is usual to find a *Pipal* tree (*Ficus religiosa*) the descendant, it may be of the *Bodh-drum* or "Tree of Knowledge," affected by the Founder of Buddhism, and perhaps a survival from some old religious system long since passed away and forgotten. The column of Prayága is similarly provided, only the tree is not now visible, being placed in a temple which the accumulated debris of ages has reduced to the condition of a catacomb: nor is it now believed to be a *Pipal*.

The sacred tree of Prayága is called *Akshay Bat*, or "undying Banian;" *Bat* being the name of a fig, but generally appropriated to the *Ficus Indica*, rather than to the *Pipal*. In the time of Hwen Thsang, the change must have already taken place, for the Chinese pilgrim (7th century after Christ) saw what was probably the present temple, though even in his time it had passed from the hands of the Buddhists, and had become a scene of the bloody rites of Shiva.

It was then a large tree with spreading branches, standing before the principal chamber of the temple. It now appears in the form of a bifurcated log in the side of the underground crypt already mentioned, and the attendant ministers say that it was placed there by one of their demi-gods, who broke off the two ends, in order to plant one at Guya, the other at Juganáth.

The entrance to the grotto is between the pillar of Asoka and the Ellenborough barracks, and consists of a passage down which the visitor is conducted by an attendant with a lighted torch. The courtyard, if it may be so called, to which this passage yields, is square, and in the centre is a *linga*, the phallic emblem sacred to Máhádeva or Shiva. In the cloisters on the sides of the quadrangle are the shrines of the gods, faintly illuminated by the light of the torch. The walls drip with a scanty moisture, said by the Hindus to be the trace of the hidden river Sarsuti—the Arethusa mentioned above—in her way to join her less modest sisters at the Tirbeni.

The following are Cunningham's remarks:—

"I think there can be little doubt that the famous tree here described by the Chinese pilgrim is the well known *Akshay Bat*, or "undecaying Banian tree," which is still an object of worship at Allahabad. This tree is now situated underground at one side of a pillared court, which would appear to have been open formerly, and which is, I believe, the remains of the temple described by Hwen Thsang. The temple is situated inside the fort of Allahabad to the east of the Ellenborough Barracks, and due north from the stone pillar of Asoka and Samudra Gupta. Originally both tree and temple must have been on the natural ground level; but from the constant accumulation of rubbish they have been gradually earthed up until the whole of the lower portion of the temple has disappeared underground. The upper portion has long ago been removed, and the only access to the *Akshay Bat* now available is by a flight of steps which leads down to a square pillared courtyard. This court has apparently once been open to the sky, but it is now closed in to secure darkness and mystery for the holy Fig tree.

"The *Akshay Bat* is next mentioned by Rashid-ud-din in the *Jamiut-towarikh*, in which he states that the "tree of *Prâg*" is situated at the confluence of the Jumna and Ganges. As most of his information was derived from *Abu Rihân*, the date of this notice may with great probability be referred to the time of Mahmud of Ghazni. In the 7th century a great sandy plain, two miles in circuit, lay between the city and the confluence of the rivers, and as the tree was in the midst of the city, it must have been at least one mile from the confluence. But nine centuries later, in the beginning of Akbar's reign, Abdul Kâdir speaks of the 'tree from which people cast themselves into the river.'* From this statement I infer that, during the long period that intervened between the time of Hwen Thsang and that of Akbar, the two rivers had gradually carried away the whole of the great sandy plain, and had so far encroached upon the city as to place the holy tree on the very brink of the water. Long before this time the old city had no doubt been deserted, for we know that the fort of *Ilâhâbâs* was founded on its site in the 21st year of Akbar's reign, that is, in A.H. 982, or A.D. 1572. Indeed, the way in which Abu Rihân speaks of the 'tree' instead of the city of Prâg, leads me to believe that the city itself had already been deserted before his time. As far as I am aware, it is not once mentioned in any Muhammadan history until it was refounded by Akbar."†

The General has made a miscalculation as to the Christian era: the 21st year of Akbar was not 1572 but 1575-6. The Emperor was then engaged in the struggle with Daud Khan of Jaunpore, by which the Afghan dynasty of the "Kings of the East" was finally overthrown; and no doubt saw the advantages of a place of arms at the head of the Doab in the same light as the Kshatris of old and the British of to-day. Mythology was also called into the service of the wise and eclectic Emperor. It was said that his Majesty was in some sort a child of the sacred confluence. A holy man of the Hindus, named Makund Brahmachari—so runs the tale — burned himself at the Tirbeni in order to be born again as the son of Humaiun. A modern historian (*Miftah-ul-Towarik*) says that a copper-plate, with an inscription commemorative of this miracle, was extant down to comparatively recent times.

---

* Elliot's Muhammadan Historians of India, p. 243.

† Reinaud Fragments Arabs, &c., p. 103, and Dowson's Elliot, I., 55.

Another legend of the time is thus related by Cunningham :—

"According to the common tradition of the people, the name of Prayâga was derived from a Brahman, who lived during the reign of Akbar. The story is that when the Emperor was building the fort, the walls on the river face repeatedly fell down in spite of all the precautions taken by the architect. On consulting some wise men, Akbar was informed that the foundations could only be secured by being laid in human blood. A proclamation was then made, when a Brahman, called Prayâga, voluntarily offered his life on the condition that the fort should bear his name. This idle story, which is diligently related to the pilgrims who visit the *Akshay Bat*, may at least serve one useful purpose in warning us not to place too much faith in these local traditions. The name of *Prayâga* is recorded by Hwen Thsang in the 7th century, and is, in all probability, as old as the reign of Asoka, who set up the stone pillar about B.C. 240, while the fort was not built until the end of the 16th century."

Such then is the capital of the North-West Provinces, a tract nearly coincident with the old province of Hindustan. Though neither central in situation, nor important as a commercial mart, its strategic value is great, and the money that has been sunk on the public offices will always render it a matter of serious consideration to depose it from its eminence as a provincial metropolis.

CAWNPORE.

NOTES ON CAWNPORE.

The Cawnpore Railway Station, one of the first that was completed in Upper India, is at the same time one of the best and most convenient. The traveller will here find comfortable shelter in Mr. Kelner's rooms, and excellent carriages to convey him, after rest and refreshment, to the Civil and Military Stations. The city is by no means inconsiderable, being a flourishing *entrepôt* of trade, commanding the navigation of the Ganges, and forming the terminal junction of the Lucknow Branch of the Oudh and Rohilkund Railway. It contains a population of about 1,16,450 inhabitants, but has no buildings of sufficient importance to detain a visitor.

It is in the Cantonments and Civil Lines that the objects of interest will be found; an interest as deep and abiding as it is mournful.

The Ganges is navigable southward to the sea, a distance of 1,000 miles, and northward to Sukhátál, a distance of 300, the traffic being principally carried on by means of heavy-looking native barges propelled by oars and sails; though a train of flats drawn by a steamer of small draught would probably be found more remunerative were there a Company of sufficient capital to set such an enterprise going and work it economically. A bridge of pontoons crosses the river, shortly to be replaced by the permanent high-level bridge, which is being constructed for the State Railway. The Ganges Canal also here discharges itself into the river, from which it had been taken, more than 400 miles higher up, at Hardwar. This is not the place to describe this colossal work, embracing with its distributing channels, a waterway of over 800 miles, and provided throughout with locks, falls, and bridges of the most substantial character, and bordered through its whole distance by a well-planted road.

Leaving the Railway the visitor passes by the "palatial" barracks built for the accommodation of the British Infantry; and can either drive to the right, towards the Memorial Church, or to the left, by the Canal and Gardens according as his destination be the Military or the Civil Station. Both of these stations are well-wooded, and have excellent macadamised roads, and abundance of well-built bungalows surrounded by good and productive gardens.

The place is unknown in early history, its first importance dating from A.D. 1777 when it was chosen as the seat of the advanced British garrison. This force was here posted under the treaty made by the majority of Warren Hastings' Council with the successor of the late Nawab Shuja-ood-Daolah. Mr. Hastings had been blamed for lending the support of a British Brigade to this Chief; and he was to undergo still more severe censure on the same account. Nevertheless, his censors made a very similar engagement, supplying the new Nawáb with troops, but extorting a fresh contribution from him on the occasion, together with the cession of the province of Benares.

Cawnpore was selected as the Head-quarters of the British force with excellent military and political judgment. Not only is it well-situated in itself, but its position formed the key of the border line, which divided the then British frontier from the province of Oudh, as also from those under the direct sway of the tottering throne of the Great Moghul. It is about 500 feet above the level of the sea; and is in latitude 26° 28′; longitude 80° 25. The distance from Calcutta is 628 miles, and from Dehli 266.

WHEELER'S ENTRENCHMENT.

Turning first, then, to the right hand, we enter the Cantonments; when the first object that meets the eye on passing the barracks is a red-brick church without windows, and a lofty pointed belfry. This is the building that marks the site of "Wheeler's entrenchment," the frail bulwark that for three weeks served as the only protection of the unhappy garrison that took up their quarters there on the mutiny of the native troops on the 6th June 1857.

The garrison of Cawnpore, under the command of Sir Hugh Massey Wheeler, consisted of the following European force :—

Artillery, one Battery of 6 guns with 59 men.
Infantry, 60 men, H. M.'s 84th.
„ 74 invalids, H. M.'s 32nd.
„ 15 of 1st Madras Fusiliers.

The native troops consisted of the 2nd Cavalry, the 1st, 53rd, and 56th N.I., and the native gunners attached to the battery. The whole number of the European population, including Civil, Railway, Canal, and other Staffs, is estimated at about 750 souls. "There was at the time" to use the words of Mr. J. W. Sherer (from whose report these figures are derived), "residing at Bithoor," a village a little farther up the Ganges, "a Hindoo of rank named Doondhoo Punth, but commonly called *Nana Sahib*. . . . He was the adopted son of Bajee Rao" (the last Peishwa or head of the Mahratta confederacy) "and inherited his houses, landed property, jewels, &c." This man had a grievance which, in the usual unsympathetic way of prosperous masters, the British had wholly failed to appreciate. Adopted in 1832 he had been brought up to look upon himself as heir to the Peishwaship, a barren honor no doubt, yet preserving that character of personal distinction so flattering to all barbarians. Five years before the mutiny old Bajee Rao died; and the government of Lord Dalhousie at once announced that the titular dignity had ceased, and that the adoptive heir would only inherit the private property; the pension and salute being discontinued, and some old pieces of artillery withdrawn which had contributed to a sort of child's play of regality in the declining years of the captive potentate. For the next four years Doondhoo Punth had spared no exertion to persuade the Court of Directors to revoke this decision and his failure constituted a deep offence. His motto now seemed to be taken from mouth of Virgil's baffled goddess :—

Flectere si nequeo superos Acheronta movebo.

And he proceeded " to raise Hell" with a vengeance.

On the morning of the 6th June, the native troops mutinied, though without following the custom then prevalent of murdering their officers. They marched out to Kalianpur, the first stage on the Dehli road, evidently with the intention of joining the main body of the mutineers who were trying to strike a blow for some not very intelligible cause in the old Moghul Capital.

In the meanwhile Sir Hugh Wheeler had taken his followers, combatant and non-combatant, into the refuge that he had prepared for them in the depôt-barracks, standing where the new church is now to be seen. These consisted of two long barracks, of one story each, and each built for the accommodation of one company. One was thatched, and both were surrounded by flat-roofed verandah: the inner walls were of brick, a foot and a half in thickness. In the neighbourhood stood the usual out-offices and a well, which is still to be seen bearing the marks of round-shot. About this slender shelter a trench had been dug and the earth thrown up on the outside so as to form a rude parapet about five feet in height: the guns looked through openings left for the purpose, and were entirely without protection. The whole was about 200 yards square, armed with ten field-pieces of various small calibres. There was an insufficient stock of provisions calculated to hold out thirty days. On the other side was soon collected a force of overwhelming resources. But we must not anticipate.

It has been mentioned that the Nana was not supposed to have felt his grievances. So far from this, the superficial hospitalities of the Chief had seduced the English—easily flattered in their pride of race—into thinking that the Nana was their friend. The Magistrate and the General were both agreed on this; and the Nana was accordingly put in charge of Arsenal, Magazine, Park, and Treasury. Thus supplied his turn had come, his course was clear. Following the mutineers to Kalianpur he had little difficulty in persuading them to return and join in an attack on the British, thus striking their blow where they were instead of marching nearly three hundred miles to strike it at Delhi. On the very day that Wheeler entered the entrenchment the traitor threw off the mask and declared his intentions. On the forenoon of the 7th June, the bombardment was formally opened. Next day the flag of Islam was hoisted—even to a Brahman we may fancy, it seemed difficult to inaugurate a crusade under the phallic emblem of Siva—and an incessant fire of all arms was opened upon the ill-protected Europeans.

Looking back with post eventual wisdom one asks, why did the defenders of British power choose such a situation? In answer, Mr. Sherer points out that the troops being supposed to have marched to Delhi, a place of refuge on the Calcutta side would be most appropriate, especially with a friendly Native Chief ready to assist one to get off to Allahabad. Mr. Sherer thus argues:—General Wheeler undoubtedly acted upon the supposition that "the regiments would mutiny, and at once leave for Dehli, the great centre of revolt, and that the Nana would not take an actively hostile part against us." This opinion is justifiable. The regiments when they did at length throw of their allegiance at once marched for Delhi. There could not then have been at that time any understanding between the troops and the Nana. On the 26th of May the Nana had been called in from Bithoor by the Magistrate of Cawnpore, Mr. Hillersden, to aid in the almost hopeless work of staying the rush of the strong tide of mutiny and rebellion. He must necessarily have been cognizant of the plans which had been matured for self-defence against the anticipated onslaught. He obeyed the summons with alacrity and was apparently sincere. He brought with him two hundred of the five hundred armed retainers, and two of three guns he was permitted to have. He had then been put in charge of the Treasury, situated near his own house in Nawabgunj, and preparations to protect the European community went on. He was necessarily in consultation with the authorities both Civil and Military. He was made aware of their intentions and was acquainted with their views and resources. Probably he expressed approval of all, and concurred in the opinion that the troops, devoid of a suitable leader round whom to rally, would at once make for Dehli. So far all was well. Aided by the Nana the small devoted garrison could have passed safely down to Allahabad unmolested.

There were other reasons on which Mr. Sherer could hardly at the time enlarge, but which were no doubt very strong in the sorely-tried Councils of Cawnpore, and which involved two capital errors. It was a grievous mistake to trust to the friendship of the Nana; it was a still more grievous mistake to trust to the readiness of the Calcutta Government. As to the first all that was necessary has been said; and we have seen that the lesson has been taught to all conquerors never again to believe in the love of those that they have injured. As to the second it may be allowable to say this much more now. Lord Canning afterwards displayed fine qualities; passive courage, magnanimity, and a merciful justice. But he was not a man of quick sympathies or of keen intelligence, nor had he at the time any knowledge of the country or its people. And he was surrounded by a conclave of persons reared in the apostolical succession of mediocrity, and the seclusion from the world which too often characterize the members of a Bureau. Hence it happened that though promises of aid were freely sent to Cawnpore, the difficulties of carrying them out were not foreseen, nor the consequences of not fulfilling them appreciated. It is now known that Wheeler had been led to expect reinforcements by the 14th, only one week after the siege began: and it was necessarily thought desirable that those reinforcements should be met at the nearest possible point, without being exposed to the perils of a struggle through an unknown city filled with lawless plunderers and escaped convicts, and bad characters of all sorts. This last was probably the chief reason that decided the choice of the entrenchment; and was thus one of the causes that led to the ruin of the garrison. The possession of the treasure and of the heavy artillery by the Nana being the other.

Here, at all events, for three dreadful weeks, the feeble garrison, with their sick and dying all round, without medicines or hospital stores, and short of ammunition, were sapped, bombarded, and starved, in a climate which persons of their race usually find difficult to support with the aid of every available comfort. Still, under all trials, the spirit of the Baresark kept aflame; in numerous sallies the gallant fellows captured or spiked the enemy's guns with little or no loss to themselves; nor, though the position became utterly untenable, did the craven traitors without ever venture to assault it. Though capable, however, of guarding their lives against enemies in arms, the soldiers were powerless against other kinds of death. Reinforced as they had been by the heroic Lawrence from Lucknow, they had perhaps entered the entrenchment two hundred and fifty strong. By the third week one hundred of these were, happily for themselves, taken from the evil that was to come. Delicate women, too, and still more feeble children, the pallid offspring of exiled mothers, sank daily under sufferings which can only be partly realized by an effort of imagination. Still the brave hearts struggled on. On the 26th at length a gleam of hope dawned; the Nana offered to treat. In consequence of negotiations which followed, it was agreed that the survivors should depart under the escort of their quondam friend the Nana. It can scarcely be wondered at, that when, on that morning, the Nana offered to treat, his proposition was listened to. Contrary to the advice and remonstrances of many of the officers the treaty was agreed to.

But in truth nothing could have saved them. Their agony could not have been protracted for another three weeks' horror; and Havelock did not near Cawnpore till the 16th of July.

What was in the meantime the fate of those who (in the words of Horace) "trusted themselves to faithless foes" is written on the saddest page of British history, a page that will bear the tears of many generations of readers. The proffered terms had been accepted. Boats were provided for the conveyance of the remains of the garrison to Allahabad. On the fatal morning of the 27th of June the survivors proceeded to embark. It is not possible to dwell upon the events connected with this episode with calmness. The facts far exceeded all that the imagination could conceive. Immediately on the embarkation of the deluded and now helpless people who left the enclosure in the early dawn of the morning, there followed the most dastardly piece of treachery that has perhaps ever been perpetrated. Only a portion of the party had taken their places in the boats, when, by previous arrangement, the boatmen set the thatched coverings of the boats on fire, and rushed on to the bank. A heavy fire of grape and musketry was then opened on the Europeans. Out of thirty boats, two only managed to start; one of these was shortly swamped by round-shot, but its passengers were enabled to reach the leading boat. Of those on board the other twenty-eight boats, some were killed, some drowned, and the rest brought back prisoners. Of the fugitives who quitted their weak position but a few hours before only fifty had contrived to escape for the time, though it was in the case of the larger portion only to die shortly after. The boat they occupied was under an incessant galling fire from both banks, but it pursued its course till it grounded at the distance of six miles. All the night of that eventful and trying day continued the struggle for life, amid hopes and fears of which we can form but a very slight conception. Early on the following morning the miserable occupants of the frail bark managed to push on till the boat again grounded. They were again attacked, and a number were killed; but the assailants were driven off, and retired to Cawnpore. The Nana then immediately despatched *two complete regiments* in pursuit. As it was found impracticable to move the boat, a party of *fourteen* landed to drive back their assailants, which they did most effectually. Of those fourteen but four survived—one, now Colonel Mowbray Thompson, to tell "the story of Cawnpore;"—those left in the boat were brought back and shared the subsequent fate of all the others. Returning to the ghât we find that "the massacre continued. Musketry was kept up from behind neighbouring walls," on a paralysed body of unarmed fugitives, "and sowars made attacks on the helpless crowd by riding in amongst them, and slashing in all directions with their tulwars."

At last came the order to cease from slaughter, and the miserable survivors were driven off.

Such, in brief, is the story of "Wheeler's Entrenchment," a story of an encounter between Europe and Asia more memorable than that of Thermopylæ or the Anabasis as showing the characteristic results of different climates and civilisations. On the site now stands the Memorial Church; an edifice of considerable size and architectural pretensions. The result, however, at least so far as the exterior is concerned, is not by any means satisfactory. The style is the Romanesque, certainly much better adapted to an Indian climate than the everlasting "carpenters' gothic" one sees in almost every cantonment or Civil Station. But the walls and sky-line are painfully monotonous and unrelieved; and the belfry at one end, with its sharp-pointed finial, gives the whole outline the appearance of the head of a rhinoceros. From this general condemnation, nevertheless, must be excepted the west front, which contains some pleasing details. The entrance consists of three doorways, not perhaps of sufficient height, and objectionable on account of the too great differences of the arches not merely as to size but as to shape also; but they are crowned with a nice sloped moulding in red brick, over which is another, upright, in stone. And over this again is placed a wheel-window that is grand in its dimensions and truly fine in proportion and in ornament. This window is probably a direct transcript from the west front of some old Italian Church; but it is introduced with taste and propriety, and harmonises well with the rest of the building. The walls are of red brick, stained and pointed so as to have a mincing and artificial effect, only partially redeemed by buttresses and copings of a fine buff freestone, which is not however always well-selected; and the form of these accessories is far too untreated and insignificant.

The interior is far better than the outside; and is not open to much objection on any score, if it be only found to have light and air enough for the purposes of worship. There are no windows in the basement walls of the aisles, which are covered with monumental tablets, and separated from the nave by bold segmental arches springing from capitals well-carved in geometrical and floral patterns. But the light, besides the wheel-window, is only admitted by the clerestories above these arches and by an arcade-window in the wall of the circular apse; and it is very much to be feared that when all these openings have been filled, as is the intention, with painted glass, there will be, in the body of the Church, a "darkness visible" which will render the use of "long primer" prayerbooks indispensable, even for the youngest eyes in the congregation.

Such as it is, the Memorial Church is a *cheap* building, the whole cost to completion being only stated as about £18,500. The chancel floor is of Minton's glazed tiles, and all the interior decoration is in good taste and very creditable to the judgment, care and industry of Mr. Cleburne, the District Engineer, by whom this portion of the work has been carried out. Whether or no a Church was the most appropriate or durable memorial of the sufferings of that sorrowful time, certain it is that some such record was felt to be required. In no spirit of vengeance, but with a feeling of pity for the past, and of good intentions for the future, let us leave the relics of the brave in the House of Prayer.

THE SCENE OF THE FINAL MASSACRE.

Crossing the Canal we come upon the Civil Station, in which there is little worthy of remark excepting the garden which surrounds the scene of the third Act in the tragedy of Fifty-seven.

We have seen the close of the second; the four resolute men borne down the broad Ganges; the other survivors of the massacre at Suttee Chowra Ghât driven, scared and famished, towards the quarters of the Nana. Wearied with slaughter the palled ruffians placed their female and ungrown victims for the time in a building called the *Savada Kotee*, not far from the

Railway Station. The rest of the male captives were shot on the parade ground. About ten days later there was a general move nearer the town. The Nana took up his quarters in a house in the civil lines then occupied as a hotel; the women and children, with some few officers, who had somehow escaped or had joined from without, and been captured later, were put into a house near the bank of the river, called *Beebeeghur*. Here they were supplied with coarse food and furniture, and the women employed to grind corn.

What may have been the exact condition of these once delicately habited beings, now plunged in hopeless misery, no human heart will ever know. Whether the bitterness of trampled pride was added to that of quickly approaching death ; or whether a stunned apathy had thrown over their sufferings its natural anœsthetic, and they were left to "rot in dull obstruction" without active molestation; each one must fancy these things for himself. A Bengalee apothecary attended them for a few days, and from fragments of his diary found in the house it was afterwards learned that birth and deaths went on among them. The rest of their existence is a blank. It is satisfactory to be able to add that the enquiry held at the time satisfied Mr. Sherer that dishonor had not been added to the other horrors of those dreadful days.

Whatever were their sufferings they were not of long duration. On the 10th July, Colonel Smith, of the 10th N. I., arrived with a party of refugees of both sexes from Futtehgurh. They had come down the river in a boat, but were captured on passing Bithoor. To the number of some 55 (chiefly women and children) they were put into the palace for the night. Next morning they were compelled to march on foot, over twelve miles under the July sun, to receive sentence from the Nana at Cawnpore. Col. Smith and Mr. Thornhill the Judge, with the women and children who had accompanied them, were thrown into the *Beebeeghur* already crowded with the Cawnpore captives. The rest of the men were shot.

But the Nana's riegn of terror was drawing to a close, though not to terminate without a stroke destined to make the world shudder, and justify the pride of race which says of every unknown Asiatic:—

Hic niger est, hunc tu, Romane, caveto.

Among the Nana's most confidential advisers was one Azimoola Khan, who had risen from being a common pimp and lackey to the dignity of Private Secretary to the titular Peshwa, and had in that capacity visited Europe on behalf of his employer. How the sleek ways and bright shawls and jewels of this human tiger fascinated a class of simpletons in London and Brighton, how he spied out and overrated British weakness before Sebastopol and conspired with Britain's enemies in Turkey, this is not the place to tell. His papers were seized at Bithoor, and are now, it is believed, in private hands. The writer of these pages saw them, and they taught him that this travelled traitor had been the moving spirit in raising the insurrection against the nation at whose hands he had received so much ill-judged hospitality. He had actually been attempting to tempt distinguished ladies who had entertained him in London to visit his master in India at the very time when, taking advantage of the Persian war, he was machinating the mutiny in the interests of the Peshwa and the Moghul.

He was now to put the finishing touch to his work of mischief. The Councils of the wicked were being troubled. Danger was on its way. Stories were brought in of terrible, bronzed men coming up the trunk road, before whose advance the "Bahadoors" of the Bengal army were blowing like chaff and dust before the fan of the threshing-floor. Futtehpore had fallen; on the morning of the 15th a fresh disaster happened at Aoung. Mr. Sherer's words will best describe what followed; it being premised that Azimoola probably knew just enough of the English to suppose that Havelock would continue his desperate advance so long as a child or a woman remained alive. But either it was hoped that the knowledge that they were too late would check the would-be deliverers, or it was reckoned that they would at least be paralysed in the work of punishment if all witnesses could be removed.

At all events one of the most horrible scenes in modern history followed the news of the last defeat.

"The battle of Aoung was fought early in the forenoon of the 15th [July], and the Pandoo Nuddee was forced, to the best of my recollection, by about 11 o'clock the same day. There was therefore ample time for news of the repulse, and the steady advance of the British troops to have reached Cawnpore early in the afternoon. There is every reason therefore to suppose that the fate of the unhappy captives was immediately made the subject of discussion. The decision arrived at, is now known and execrated throughout the civilized world. It was decided that the captives should be put to death. The order was carried into execution about sundown. There were four gentlemen, three of them of the Futtehgurh party, who by some mischance, or for some especial reason, had been reserved from the fate which had already fallen upon their male companions. These were first taken out of the *Beebeeghur* and murdered on the high road. Then the general massacre commenced. It seems probable, that vollies were first fired into the doors and windows, and then the executioners were sent to do the rest with swords. If the work was anything like completed, it must have taken a considerable time. At length the doors were closed and night fell upon what had happened. The hotel where the Nana had his quarters, was within fifty yards of this house, and I am credibly informed that he ordered a *nautch*, and passed the evening with singing and dancing. Early next morning, orders were given for the *Beebeeghur* to be cleared. There must have been near upon 200 corpses. So many, I do not think, could have been thrown into the well. It seems probable, that a portion were dragged down to the Ganges. Considering the smallness of the house, and the crowded condition of the captives, it is next to impossible that all can have been slaughtered the previous night. It is exercising therefore no morbid imagination and pandering to no prurient curiosity to say that I hold no doubt some of the living met a more terrible death than assassination even, by being plunged with their dead companions into the tainted waters of the well."—(*Sherer's Report.*)

Such is Mr. Sherer's simple narrative, written shortly after the event, with the evidence of eye-witnesses before him. More it is not perhaps well that we should know: more, at least, will never be known with certainty. The following graphic words complete the picture. After relating how he rode into the city with two troopers announcing the restoration of order, Mr. Sherer thus proceeds:—

"Thence we were directed to the *Beebeeghur* and well. And then broke upon our eyes that dreadful spectacle over the very idea of which there are still broken spirits and widowed hearts mourning terror-stricken in distant England. . . . . There were no dead bodies, except in the well. The well was narrow and deep; and, looking down, you could only see a tangled mass of human limbs entirely without clothing. To the best of my belief there was not a word written on the walls."

Shortly after the restoration of order, Lord Canning resolved that a fitting monument should be erected, whereby he might mark the scene of these frightful sorrows, and honor "the unhappy dust he could not save." With this object Mr. C. B. Thornhill, the then Commissioner of the Division, who had lost two brothers in the disturbances, was commanded to devise and superintend the construction of a work that should protect the fatal well and otherwise distinguish and preserve the site; while at the Viceroy's own cost, the statue was ordered from Baron Marochetti, then in the bloom of Court favor, and of at least a temporary popularity. Not long after Mr. G. E. Lance, who had succeeded Mr. Sherer in charge of the district, undertook to lay out the surrounding plain as a Memorial Garden. The result is not wholly satisfactory, perhaps, in any respect. The statue is monotonous and unmeaning in design, rough and inartistic in execution. Nothing can well be conceived more commonplace than the Carpenter's gothic of the surrounding wall, with its frivolous crocketted battlements, purposeless finials, and tedious rows of lancet-windows with their dull trefoiled mullions. The ogee doorway and cast-iron doors are the only decent feature, and they were designed, it is believed, by Col. H. Yule of the Royal Engineers; but, seeing that the building is without a roof, there does not seem any purpose in a door. It is on a scroll over this portal that we read the touching inscription "these are they which came out of great tribulation." It is a pity the rest of the monument is not more worthy of this really fine opening. The garden is well laid out, and generally in good order; but it is much too large for the enclosure of a tomb. There is no other place of the kind in Cawnpore; yet the necessary observances of a cemetery render this large and ornamental piece of ground useless for the ordinary purposes of a public garden; even though the monument is not visible from any but the most central portion. If this portion and the pretty, creeper-grown graveyards that it contains were railed off, the remaining garden might well be utilised for the behoof of the living, without derogating from the respect due to the dead. Native visitors, long excluded, are now admitted to the garden by passes readily given to men of known respectability.

INDUSTRIES, &c.

Before leaving Cawnpore the visitor will perhaps desire some information regarding the chief manufactures for which it is becoming celebrated.

The town has long been favourably known for the skill and enterprise of its native saddlers; and the cheap and efficient articles of this trade that can be turned out will doubtless surprise those who have never before seen them. Owing to these circumstances the Government has established a manufactory of its own, which—at present under the able superintendence of Colonel T. Stewart, R.A.—tans and works up leather into harness and half-mountings for the use of the Bengal Army. The premises are on the river-side, and well worthy of a visit from any one provided with due introduction.

The preparation of cotton-yarns and piece-goods is also assuming considerable importance. The Elgin Mills, established in 1864, are now possessed of 13,000 spindles and 150 looms in working order, giving employment to 312 adult males, 34 women, and 220 boys.

From the commencement of this year these mills are destined to encounter a formidable rival in the form of a new factory.

called "The Muir Mills," which are starting with a good prospectus, from which a few extracts may be made.

"The Company is organized to erect Spinning and Weaving Mills at Cawnpore, with ten thousand spindles and one hundred power-looms, for the purpose of manufacturing the coarser descriptions of twists and cloths suitable for the use of Natives, military and police clothing, and tent-making, for which there is an unlimited demand throughout the country.

"The Twists will comprise 40's, 30's, and 20's Mule, and the Cloths, Dhoties, Shirtings, Madapollams, T. Cloth, Dussotie, Indigo Press Cloth, and American Drills. The above have all been tried and found very successful at the Elgin Mills, Cawnpore. It is intended to make Sheeting for the Troops also.

* * * * *

"The out-turn from ten thousand spindles and one hundred power-looms is estimated as follows:—

10,000 spindles turning out average No. 25's at 16 ozs. per spindle per week of 60 hours = lbs. 10,000, multiplied by 50 working weeks per annum, = lbs. 5,00,000.

Cost of the above lbs. 5,00,000 Yarn.

Cotton 5,00,000 lbs., plus 15 per cent. waste, = 5,75,000 lbs., at 4 annas per lb. =	Rs.	1,43,750	0	0
Manufacturing charges at 2½ ans. per lb. on 5,00,000 lbs. =	„	78,125	0	0
Total cost,	Rs.	2,21,875	0	0

RETURNS.

Value of lbs. 3,50,000 Twist, average No. 25's, at 9½ ans. per lb. ...	Rs.	2,07,812	8	0
Value of lbs. 1,50,000 Cloth, at 10½ ans. per lb.	„	98,437	8	0
Value of lbs. 50,000 waste at 2 ans. per lb.	„	6,250	0	0
	Rs.	3,12,500	0	0
Deduct cost brought down,	„	2,21,875	0	0
Profits,	Rs.	90,625	0	0

Being equal to 22·656 per cent. on four lakhs capital."

THE RAILWAY BRIDGE.

Since these sheets were sent to Press, the Iron Lattice Bridge, referred to in the commencement, has been completed and tested. The following figures will be found interesting. I am indebted for them to the courtesy of S. B. Newton, Esq., the Resident Engineer in charge of the work.

Length of bridge 25 spans of 110 ft.	} Total = 2,830 running ft.		
Ditto 2 do. 40 ft.			
Girders	ditto		ditto
Average depth of foundation wells below low-water mark ...	} 60 feet.		
Time taken in construction ...	6 years.		

NOTE.—The bridge was commenced just before the monsoons of 1869; completion was delayed some two or three years in consequence of 8 wells falling over during monsoons, 1870, after which the piers were newly designed, and operations again commenced in 1871 on new foundations.

Approximate cost of whole work from commencement to finish, including superintendence, protection works, approaches (Oudh and Cawnpore) and all works connected therewith, say 20 lacs.

NOTE.—The bridge is provided with an upper and lower road way. All foot-passengers, horses, &c., &c., will pass through lower or sub-way. Trains and all special traffic, such as loaded Native cotton carts, camels, elephants and every thing that cannot pass through the sub-way, pass on the top. Good pucca roads are provided on each side of river to upper and lower roads.

NOTE ON MEMORIAL CHURCH.

For the benefit of those who may require details, it may be added that the cost of the Church, though intended originally to be sought for in private beneficence, has in fact, chiefly in the end been derived from the revenues of the country. Some handsome gifts, however, have been received from time to time.

H. H. the Maharaja of Jodhpur has contributed a quantity of white marble slabs for the flooring of the chancel, and a handsome brass lectern has been given by Mrs. W. C. Plowden. A memorial window has been erected by the friends of Mr. J. McKillop, who was shot in the intrenchment; it is the centre of those which adorn the apse. The E. I. R. Company employés have subscribed a fund which, after commemorating those of their body who fell in the siege, is expected to go some way towards providing for a peal of bells. But money for the completion of a good peal, and for the rest of the stained glass, is still wanting; and it is to be hoped that some visitors to the sacred scene may, from time to time, be induced to put themselves into communication with the Committee for these and similar purposes. The work is, in every sense, a national monument; and as such it should be regarded.

NOTE ON GARDENS.

As remarked in the text, the Memorial Gardens were laid out by Mr. G. E. Lance, when Magistrate of the district: a work for which he was honoured with the thanks of Government on the 24th March 1863. It has ever since been under the charge of a Committee consisting of the chief local officials, civil and military. The well and adjacent cemeteries were solemnly consecrated by the late lamented Bishop Cotton in the presence of a distinguished company, among whom were the Viceroy (Lord Elgin), H. E. Sir Hugh Rose (Lord Strathnairn), Major General Macduff, Mr. C. Thornhill, C.B. (Commissioner of the Division), and the Ven. Archdeacon Pratt. The funds for the original outlay appear to have been partly provided out of the fine levied from the citizens for misconduct in 1857, and partly from other local sources and from public money. The total area is nearly 50 acres; and the whole of the iron-work—including the large amount of iron railing required for so extensive an enclosure—was cast at the workshops of the Ganges Canal, Rurki. The total cost of the garden appears to have been about £7,000, and that of the Monument £4,000;* for the annual maintenance a grant of about £500 is made by the Government of India. The gardener first employed was Murphy, one of the four survivors who escaped by swimming down the river: he has since died. The whole area is irrigable from the canal, which accounts for the uniformly verdant appearance it presents in the midst of its arid environments.

Christ Church in the Civil Station may be also inspected. It contains monuments of the mutiny, among which are tablets to Mr. Fraser, Lieutenant Sotheby, R. A., and the officers of the 64th. It was nearly destroyed in the mutiny, and its restoration was one of the objects of the fine levied upon the city.

In the village of Gothaya, near Nawabgunj, will be found an Orphanage of the S. P. G., where are monuments of a few of the heroes of the Sepoy War; amongst others that of the gallant and accomplished Stuart Beatson of the Bengal Cavalry, who then prematurely closed a career of abundant promise. The Orphanage at present maintains one hundred and thirty children.

The following description of the present state of Cawnpore is borrowed from a letter of the *Daily News'* special correspondent in India, which appeared in October 1874:†—"The drive from the Railway Station to the European Cantonments is pleasant and shaded. At a bend in the road comes into view a broad, flat, treeless parade-ground. This plain lies within a circle of foliage, above which, on the south-eastern side, rise the balconies and flat tops of a long range of barracks built in detached blocks, while around the rest of the circle the trees shade the bungalows of the Cantonment. Near the centre of this level space is an irregular inclosure defined by a shallow sunk wall and low quickest hedge, and in the middle of this inclosure rises the ornate and not

* Exclusive of a charge—understood to be very large—of the iron-work and railings from Rurki.

† The statements are, generally, correct, but contain some small inaccuracies.

wholly satisfactory structure known as the 'Memorial Church.' It is built on the site of the old dragoon hospital, which was the very focus of the agony of the siege. The outline of the famous earthwork is almost wholly obliterated; only in places is it to be dimly recognised by brick-discolored lines, and a low raised line on the smooth maidan. The inclosure now existing has no reference to the outlines of the entrenchment. That inclosure, when entered, is found to be littered with the appliances of building, piles of bricks, puddles of mortar, and baulks of timber; for the 'Memorial Church' has lapsed into the hands of the Public Works Department, and, although seventeen years have elapsed since the tragedy and the heroism it is meant to commemorate, it is still unfinished. But, littered as it is, there is much of deep interest inside this inclosure. We come first on a railed in memorial tomb bearing an inscription in raised letters, on a cross let into the tesselated pavement. 'In three graves within this inclosure lie the remains of Major Edward Vibart, 2nd Bengal Cavalry, and about seventy officers and soldiers who, after escaping from the massacre at Cawnpore on June 27, 1857, were captured by the rebels at Sheorajpore and murdered on July 1st.' The inmates of these graves were originally buried elsewhere, and were removed hither when the inclosure was formed. In another part of the inclosure is a raised tomb, the slab of which bears the inscription 'This stone marks a spot which lay within Wheeler's entrenchment, and covers the remains and is sacred to the memory of those who were the first to meet their death when beleaguered by mutineers and rebels in June 1857.' Two only lie in this grave, Mr. Murphy and a lady who died of fever. These two perished on the first day of the siege, and had the privilege of being decently interred within the precincts of the entrenchment. After the first day of the siege there was scant leisure for funeral rites. To find the last resting place of the remaining dead of this siege we must quit the inclosure and walk across the maidan to a spot among the trees by the road side under the shadow of No. 4 barrack. There was an empty well here when the siege began; three weeks after, when the siege ended, this well contained the bodies of 250 British people. With daylight the battle raged around that sepulchre; but when the night came the slain of the day were borne thither with stealthy step and scant attendance. Now the well is filled up, and above it, inside a small, ornamental inclosure, formed by iron railings, rises a monument which bears the following inscription:—'In a well under this inclosure were laid by the bands of their fellows in suffering the bodies of men, women, and children who died hard-by during the heroic defence of Wheeler's entrenchment when beleaguered by the rebel Nana.' Below the inscription is this apposite quotation from Psalm cxli:—'Our bones are scattered at the grave's mouth, as one cutteth and cleaveth wood upon the earth. But mine eyes are unto Thee, O God the Lord.' At the corners of the flower plot are small crosses bearing individual names. One commemorates Sir George Parker, the Cantonment Magistrate; a second, Captain Jenkins; a third, Lieutenant Saunders and the men of the 84th Regiment; a fourth, Lieutenant Glanville and the men of the Madras Fusiliers.

"The Memorial Church is in the form of a cross, and when finished will be a handsome structure as regards its interior. It will always be interesting by reason of its site and of the memorial tablets on the wall of its interior. In the left transept is a tablet 'To the memory of the Engineers of the East Indian Railway, who died and were killed in the great insurrection of 1857. Erected in affectionate remembrance by their brother Engineers in the North-West Provinces.' On the left side of the nave are several tablets. One is to the memory of poor young John Nicklen Martin, killed in the boats at Suttee Chowrah Ghât. Another commemorates three officers, two sergents, two corporals, a drummer, and twenty privates of the 34th Regiment, killed at the (second) battle of Cawnpore November 28, 1857; that day on which the Gwalior Contingent, ...
made itself so unpleasant . . . .

. . . .

A third is 'To the memory of E. G. Chalwin, Bengal Light Cavalry, and his wife Louisa, who both perished during the siege of Cawnpore in July 1857. These are they which came out of great tribulation.' A fourth commemorates Captain Gordon and Lieutenant Hensley, of the 82nd Foot, also victims of the Gwalior Contingent. In the right of the nave there is a tablet 'Sacred to the memory of Philip Hayes Jackson, who, with Jane, his wife, and her brother, Ralf Blyth Croker, were massacred by rebels at Cawnpore on 27th June.' Another is to Lieutenant Angelo, of the 16th Grenadiers, Bengal Native Infantry, who also fell in the boat massacre; and a third is to the memory of the gallant Stuart Beatson, who was Havelock's Adjutant-General, and who, dying as he was of cholera, did his work at Pandoo Nuddee and Cawnpore in a dhoolie. In the right transept are tablets in memory of the officers of the Connaught Rangers and of the officers and men of the 32nd (Cornwall) Regiment, 'who fell in defence of Lucknow and Cawnpore and in the subsequent campaign'—fourteen officers and 448 'women and men.' And here, too, is perhaps the most affecting memorial of any, a tablet 'In memory of Mrs. Moore, Mrs. Wainright, Miss Wainright, Mrs. Hill, forty-three soldiers' wives, and fifty-five children murdered in Cawnpore in June 1857.'

"There are few to whom the details of that fell scene are not familiar. What a contrast between the turmoil and devilry of it and the serene calmness of the all but solitude the ghât now presents! On the knolls of the further side snug bungalows nestle among the trees, under the verandah of one of which a lady is playing with her children. The village of Suttee Chowrah, on the bluff on the left of the ghât, where Tantia Topee's sepoys were concealed, no longer exists; a pretty bungalow and its compound occupy its site. The little temple on the water's edge by the ghât is slowly mouldering into decay; on the plaster of the coping of its river wall, you may see the marks of the treacherous bullets. The stair which, built against its wall, led down to the water's edge, has disappeared. Tantia Topee's dispositions for the perpetration of the treachery could not now succeed, for the Ganges has changed its course, and there is deep water close in shore at the ghât. In the stream nearest to the Oude side, the river has cast up a long narrow island, in the fertile mud of which melons are cultivated where once whistled the shot from the guns on the Oude side of the river. A Brahmin priest is placidly sunning himself on the river platform of the temple, over the dome of which hangs the foliage of a peepul tree. A dhobie is washing the shirts of a sahib in the stream that once was dyed with the blood of the sahibs. There is no monument here of the terrible tragedy." This place, commonly known as "Slaughter Ghât," is to be found at a distance of 6¼ furlongs below the railway bridge. Mr. Simpson's description of it will be found further down.

The writer already quoted gives the following account of what he calls "the beautiful Memorial Gardens." Speaking of the foliage that forms their outer screen, he says:—"The hue of the greenery would be sombre but for the blossoms which relieve it, emblem of the Divine hope which mitigated the gloom of despair for our country-women who perished so cruelly on this spot." Of the *Beebeeghur*, the term by which among the natives is known the bungalow where the massacre was perpetrated, not one stone now remains on another, but neither its memory nor its name will be lost for all time. Natives are strolling in the shady flower-bordered walks of the Memorial Gardens, the prohibition which long debarred their entrance having been wisely removed.* In the centre of the garden rises, fringed with cypresses, a low mound, the summit of which is crowned by a circular screen, or border, of light and beautiful open work architecture. The circular space inclosed is sunk, and from the centre of this sunk space there rises a pedestal on which stands the marble presentment of an angel. There is no need to explain what episode in the tragic story this monument commemorates; the inscription round the capital of the pedestal tells its tale succinctly indeed, but the words burn, 'Sacred,' it runs 'to the perpetual memory of the great company of Christian people, chiefly women and children, who near this spot were cruelly

* It will be seen from the statement on p. 43, that this is only partially correct.

massacred by the followers of the rebel Nana Dhoondoo Punth of Bithoor; and cast the dying with the dead, into the well below on the 15th day of July 1857.' A few paces to the north-west of the monument is the spot where stood the bungalow in which the massacre was done; and now, where the sight they saw maddened our countrymen seventeen years ago to a frenzy of revenge there bloom roses and violets. And a step further on, in a thicket of arbor, vitœ trees, and cypresses, is the 'Memorial Churchyard,' with its many nameless mounds, for here were buried not a few who died during the long occupation of Cawnpore, and in the combats around it. Here there is a monument to Mr. Thornhill, the Judge of Futtehgurh, Mary his wife, and their two children, who perished in the massacre. Mr. Thornhill was one of the men brought out from the bungalow and shot earlier in the afternoon than the women's time came. Another monument bears this inscription:—'Sacred to the memory of the women and children of the 32nd, this monument is raised by twenty men of the same regiment, who were passing through Cawnpore, November 21, 1857.' An officer who formerly belonged to the company lays a stone to the memory of the women and children of the first company 61st Bengal Infantry, and among the tombstones are those of gallant Douglas Campbell of the 78th, Woodford of the second Battalion, Rifle Brigade, and Young of the 4th Bengal Native Infantry.

The well-known travelling artist, Mr. William Simpson, was in India two or three years after the massacre. He made sketches showing the appearance, at that time, both of the well at Cawnpore and the Slaughter Ghât. He writes of them as follows:—

"On my visiting the well in 1860 it remained in the same condition as at the time of the massacre. It was an ordinary brick well, similar to those common in that and other parts of India. The mouth was circular, and built a foot or two above the surface of the ground. The portion not occupied by the bodies had been filled up with earth, and was then built over level with the mouth. But in 1860, three years after the event, the decay of the bodies had caused the top to sink a few inches. At one side was the small Jona cross, of red sandstone, erected in memory of the women and children of the 32nd Regiment. This monument is shown in the Illustration. There was another flat stone, but not seen in my sketch, on the other side. It bore the following inscription:—'Secred to the memory of the women and children of the late ill-fated 1st Company, 6th Battalion, Bengal Artillery, who were slaughtered near this spot by the mutineers, on July 16, 1857.' This monument is erected by a non-commissioned officer who formerly belonged to the 1st Company, 6th Battalion. 'Spare thy people, O Lord; and give not thine heritage to reproach, that the heathen should rule over them; wherefore should they say among the people, where is there God?' Joel ii, 17. 'Fear not O land; be glad and rejoice; for the Lord will do great things.' Joel ii, 21.

"At that time, in 1860, it was under consideration what to do with the spot. A commemorative church was one of the proposals, but this was given up. At last it was settled that the well should be built over and the place inclosed. Colonel Yule, of the Bengal Engineers, produced a design for a screen in Gothic, octagonal in plan, which was approved of and carried out. Lord and Lady Canning (Lord Canning had been Governor-General during the time of the mutiny) commissioned at their own expense, Baron Marochetti to produce a figure in white marble. The top of the well having been covered over with a structure of ornamental design formed the base for this statue,—the Angel of Pity. The space around, for some distance, was laid out as a public garden, and is now the promenade of Cawnpore.

"The Slaughter Ghât at Cawnpore, as I saw it in 1860, is shown in another sketch. This was known before as the Suttee Chowrah Ghât till the fearful event of 1857 had fixed upon it the now historical appellation of 'The Slaughter Ghât.' It is on the south side of Cawnpore, and in this view the spectator is looking down the Ganges. A path led from Wheeler's entrenchment almost straight to this point, passing under the wall of the temple. By this the victims were marched to be embarked in the boats, large native barges, the same as those seen in my sketch. To the south of the temple are gardens with places on the banks to raise water from the river for irrigation. All along here men were concealed, who at a given signal, as soon as the embarkation commenced, began the murderous fusillade, from which four men only escaped. An order had been given to spare the women, who were marched away to a house near the well, where they remained till their slaughter, which followed some weeks later."

The annexed remarks set at rest on the best authority the oft-repeated error that the Nana was an English speaking native on terms of intimacy with the European Society of Cawnpore. The notion is contradicted by Mr. M. Court, formerly Magistrate, or Sub-Prefect of the District, in a letter addressed to a London paper at the time when it was supposed by some that this great malefactor had been captured. Mr. Court on that occasion wrote expressing his doubts as to the identity, and then proceeded to these interesting particulars:—"Disgusted at the deprivation by Lord Dalhousie of his salute, as heir of the Peishwas, or of any salute, he shut himself up in his palace at Bithoor, and the only Europeans he ever saw were the Magistrate of the District, the Commissioner of the Division, or other official who was under obligation since the abolition of the Resident's office, to visit him periodically. These and the Civil Surgeon were the only Europeans he saw during the year and a half when I was the Magistrate of the District. The Nana would not move to pay his respects to the Viceroy even, because deprived of his salute. He lived, it may be correctly said in the room which the Peshwa Bajee Rao died, and in which the Nana kept in veneration the bed on which the Peishwa breathed his last.

"That the Nana never entertained Europeans I do not assert. About November there was a religious *melah*, or fair, and the Nana has provided entertainment for the European visitors in the house which was in former times 'The Residency:' but the Nana never appeared as host. Baba Butt or Bala Rao represented him."

LUCKNOW.

ADVERTISEMENT.

THE following Notes are chiefly founded on official records, old Calcutta Reviews, and published histories. Reference has also been made to a recent illustrated publication, *The Lucknow Album*, the arrangement of which has been, indeed, generally followed, so that the two books may be used together. Mr. Brown's *Lucknow Guide* has also been frequently consulted.

NOTES ON LUCKNOW

WITH AN

INTRODUCTORY ACCOUNT OF THE PROVINCE OF OUDH.

Before proceeding to details as to the city and European quarters, it may be as well to give a brief description of the Province of which Lucknow is the capital.

The modern Oudh, comprising about one-half of the original *Subah* or satrapy, contains four Divisions, or Commissionerships, and the total area is 26,131 square miles (about half the area of England), of which about 21,000 are culturable, though scarcely 13,000 are actually under cultivation. The roads measure 4,500 miles, and there are 289 miles of railway open; there is also a certain amount of water-communication. The soil is productive, and the climate, though variable, not unfriendly to men, animals, and vegetation. The total average rainfall in the year is over thirty inches; the Sultanpore Division showing the most wet, and that of Hardui the least. The population is thus shown by the last census, being 476 to the square mile.

Christian.	Hindu.	Musulman.	Others.	Total.
7,761	9,881,840	1,284,436	633	11,174,670

The receipts under the head of "Imperial Revenue" are a little over one and a half million of pounds sterling, chiefly derived from the realisation of the Governmental demand on the land; of this about one-third disbursed on local purposes, and the rest a balance in favor of the Treasury. From this however must be deducted further the share of the Province in respect of all charges for Imperial works of protection and distribution—such as the Army and the Public Works—which leaves a nett gain to the Empire of something over half a million of pounds sterling per annum. Besides this the people pay about seventy-five thousand pounds in the form of local rates and cesses; but these, together with other sources of local income, and a small grant from the Treasury may be said, broadly, to be all spent on local purposes of administration.

The Province is a part of the alluvial valley of the Ganges, and of some of its tributaries, mostly coming into the Ganges by way of the Gumti, elsewhere mentioned as the river on which Lucknow stands. These form the drainage of the sub-Himalayan ranges of Nipál. The northern portion is chiefly forest; but part of this belt has been cleared, and supports a sparse pastoral and agricultural population; the soil, being humid, is generally unhealthy and better suited for pasturing cattle than for anything else. The general character of the remainder of the soil is two-fold; that on the left bank of the Gumti being mostly sandy and dry, while that between the Gumti and the Ganges is a fine fertile delta, generally irrigated from easily constructed wells.

The two principal towns of this Province are Lucknow and Faizabad. The former is the main subject of our handbook. Of the latter the following particulars may be found useful:—

Faizabad is situated on the right bank of the Ghagra, the largest Oudh affluent of the Ganges, in latitude 26° 47′; longitude 82° 10′: it is 89 miles east from Lucknow, and about 95 north from Allahabad, and is one of the stations of the Oudh and Rohilkund Railway. Five miles off is Ajudhia, the old Hindu city, from which the Province is, by a Persian corruption, named; and the two places together extend ten miles along the river, and two miles inland. Ajudhia is the site of one of the oldest cities in India: here was the capital of the kingdom of Kosala, "with strong walls, gates, and a garrison of archers, a magnificent palace, and all the paraphernalia of sovereignty." Here was born the hero Ráma, son of the Rajah Dasaratha; and the story of his sorrows, adventures, and ultimate glory forms the subject of the Rámáyana, one of the most popular of Indian poems, and now rendered acceptable to English readers in the learned yet graceful version of Mr. R. Griffith. It is not however to be supposed that any remains of those mythologic times can now be traced.

The following description of Ajudhia is taken from the Report of the Archæological Survey for 1862-3, vol. 1, p. 321:—

"The present city of Ajudhya, which is confined to the north-east corner of the old site, is just two miles in length by about three-quarters of a mile in breadth; but not one-half of this extent is occupied by buildings, and the whole place wears a look of decay. There are no high mounds of ruins, covered with broken statues and sculptured pillars, such as mark the sites of other ancient cities, but only a low irregular mass of rubbish heaps, from which all the bricks have been excavated for the houses of the neighbouring city of Faizabad. This Muhammadan city, which is two miles and-a-half in length, by one mile in breadth, is built chiefly of materials extracted from the ruins of Ajudhya. The two cities together occupy an area of nearly six square miles, or just about one-half of the probable size of the ancient Capital of Râma. In Faizabad the only building of any consequence is the stuccoed brick tomb of the old Bhao Begam, whose story was dragged before the public during the famous trial of Warren Hastings. Faizabad was the capital of the first Nawabs of Oudh, but it was deserted by Asaf-ud-daolah in A.D. 1775.

"According to the Râmâyana, the city of Ayodhya was founded by Manu, the progenitor of all mankind. In the time of Dasaratha, the father of Râma, it was fortified with towers and gates, and surrounded by a deep ditch. No traces of these works now remain, nor is it likely, indeed, that any portion of the old city should still exist, as the *Ayodhya* of Râma is said to have been destroyed after the death of *Vrihadbala* in the great war about B.C. 1426, after which it lay deserted until the time of Vikramâditya. According to popular tradition this Vikramâditya was the famous Sâkâri Prince of Ujain, but as the Hindus of the present day attribute the acts of all Vikramas to this one only, their opinion on the subject is utterly worthless. We learn, however, from Hwen Thsang that a powerful Prince of this name was reigning in the neighbouring city of Srâvasti, just one hundred years after Kanishka, or close to 78 A.D., which was the initial year of the *Sâke era* of *Sâlivâhana.* As this Vikramâditya is represented as hostile to the Buddhists, he must have been a zealous Brahmanist, and to him therefore I would ascribe the re-building of Ayodhya and the restoration of all the holy places referring to the history of Râma. Tradition says that when Vikramâditya came to Ayodhya, he found it utterly desolate and overgrown with *jangal*, but he was able to discover all the famous spots of Râma's history by measurements made from Lakshman Ghât on the *Sarju*, according to the statements of ancient records. He is said to have erected 360 temples, on as many different spots, sacred to *Râma*, and *Sitâ* his wife, to his brothers *Lakshmana*, *Bharata*, and *Satrughna*, and to the monkey god *Hanumâna.* The number of 360 is also connected with *Sâlivâhana*, as his clansman the *Bais Rajputs* assert that he had 360 wives.

"There are several very holy Brahmanical temples about Ajudhya, but they are all of modern date, and without any architectural pretensions whatever. But there can be no doubt that most of them occupy the sites of more ancient temples that were destroyed by the Musulmâns. Thus *Râmkot*, or *Hanumân Garhi*, on the east side of the city, is a small walled fort surrounding a modern temple on the top of an ancient mound. The name Râmkot is certainly old, as it is connected with the traditions of the *Mani-Parbat*, which will be hereafter mentioned; but the temple of Hanumân is not older than the time of Aurangzib. Râm Ghât, at the north-east corner of the city, is said to be the spot where Râma bathed, and *Sargdwâri* or

Swargadwâri, the "Gate of Paradise." On the north-west is believed to be the place where his body was burned. Within a few years ago there was still standing a very holy Banyan tree, called *Asok Bat*, or the "Griefless Banyan," a name which was probably connected with that of *Swargadwâri*, in the belief that people who died or were burned at this spot were at once relieved from the necessity of future births. Close by is the *Lakshman* Ghât, where his brother Lakshman bathed, and about one-quarter of a mile distant, in the very heart of the city, stands the *Janam Asthân*, or "Birth-place temple" of Râma. Almost due west, and upwards of five miles distant, is the *Guptâr* Ghât, with its group of modern white-washed temples. This is the place where Lakshman is said to have disappeared, and hence its name of *Guptâr*, from *Gupta*, which means "hidden or concealed." Some say that it was Râma who disappeared at this place, but this is at variance with the story of his cremation at *Swargadwâri*.

"The only remains at Ajudhya that appear to be of any antiquity, are three earthen mounds to the south of the city, and about a quarter of a mile distant. These are called *Mani-Parbat*, *Kuber-Parbat*, and *Sugrib-Parbat*. The first, which is nearest to the city, is an artificial mound, 65 feet in height, covered with broken bricks and blocks of *kankar*. The old bricks are eleven inches square and three inches thick. At 46 feet above the ground on the west side, there are the remains of a curved wall faced with *kankar* blocks. The mass at this point is about 40 feet thick, and this was probably somewhat less than the size of the building which once crowned this lofty mound. According to the Brahmans the *Mani-Parbat* is one of the hills which the monkeys made use of when assisting Râma. It was accidently dropped here by Sugriva, the monkey-king of *Kishkindhya*. But the common people, who know nothing of this story, say that the mound was formed by the labourers shaking their baskets on this spot every evening on their return home from the building of Râmkot. It is therefore best known by the name of *Jhowa-Jhâr* or *Ora Jhâr*, both of which mean "basketshakings." A similar story is told of the large mounds near Banâras, Nimsâr, and other places.

"Five hundred feet due south from the large mound stands the second mound called *Kuber-Parbat*, which is only 28 feet in height. The surface is an irregular heap of brick rubbish, with numerous holes made by the people in digging for bricks, which are of large size, 11 inches by 7¼ by 2. It is crowned by two old tamarind trees, and is covered with *jangal*. Close by on the south-west there is a small tank, called *Ganes-Kund* by the Hindus, and *Husen Kund* or *Imâm Talao* by the Musulmâns, because their *Tâzias* are annually deposited in it. Still nearer on the south-east there is a large oblong mound called *Sugrib-Parbat*, which is not more than 8 or 10 feet above the ground level. It is divided into two distinct portions; that to the north being upwards of 300 feet square at top, and the other to the south upwards of 200 feet. In the centre of the larger enclosure there is a ruined mound containing bricks 8½ inches square, and in the centre of the smaller mound there is a well.

"Between the *Mani* and *Kuber* mounds there is a small Muhammadan enclosure, 64 feet long from east to west, and 47 feet broad, containing two brick tombs, which are attributed to *Sis Paighambar* and *Ayub Paighambar*, or the "prophets Seth and Job." The first is 17 feet long, and the other 12 feet. These tombs are mentioned by Abul Fazl, who says—"Near this city are two sepulchral monuments, one seven and the other six cubits in length. The vulgar pretend that they are the tombs of Seth and Job, and they relate wonderful stories of them." This account shows that since the time of Akbar, the tomb of Seth must have increased in length from 7 cubits, or 10½ feet, to 17 feet through the frequent repairs of pious Musulmâns."

To the north-west of Ajudhia the first Nawáb, or Administrator, of Oudh constructed a palace about the year 1730 A.D., and for a generation and a half it continued to form the head-quarters of the *Subah*. Under the name of Faizábád Shujá-ud-Daulah added to the palace, at the same time enlarging the market-place of the town, strengthening the wall with a ditch, and round towers, and attracting a very considerable population. But when, in 1774, the British aided this Nawáb to conquer the Rohillas at the battle of Fattahganj, the accession of territory to the westward which followed disposed Shujá to seek a more central metropolis. His successor completed the transfer, a very wise one, and became the founder of modern Lucknow. Since that time Faizábád has greatly decayed; and the population and its industries have constantly drifted to Lucknow.

The following historical notes may assist the traveller in taking an interest in the Province and its modern capital:—

In the reign of the Emperor Mahomed Sháh (about the middle of the last century), a mercantile adventurer named Saádat Ali Khán—said to have been of an esteemed family of Naishápur in Persia—came to seek his fortune at the Moghul Court of Dehli. Being a man of enterprise and ability he rose in those troublous times, and succeeded the old Turkmán noble known to the English as "Nizam" in the administration of the Province of Oudh. In his time the Province was about one-fourth larger than it is now. Rohilkund indeed was not at that time included in its area, though much coveted by the Subahdár: the chief difference in the boundary was to the eastward, where it embraced what are now the Districts of Azimgarh and Gorakpur.

Saádat Ali, though living as has been seen at Faizábád, did not neglect Lucknow altogether; and the town, in his time, received considerable extension and improvement. He was succeeded in 1743 by his son Abul Mansúr Khán, known as Safdar Jang ("Piercer of Battle-ranks"), whose tomb is one of the larger monuments of Dehli. Although in the weakness of the decaying Empire, the *Subah* had thus become in a manner hereditary, it must not be supposed that Safdar Jang was in an sense regarded as an independent ruler. On the contrary he commanded the imperial forces, or intrigued for the presidency of the Cabinet, just like any other powerful and ambitious subject noble. His son Shujá-ud-Daulah succeeded to his power on his death in 1753; and in his time the Vazirate or Prime-Ministership also became hereditary in the family. The wars and adventures of this Nawáb are constantly mentioned in histories of British India; and the strange story of his death will be found in a work by the present writer on the fall of the Moghul Empire. He was succeeded by Ásaf-ud-Daulah, his son, in 1775; and from that era dates the grandeur of Lucknow. Before quitting this branch of the subject, it may be right to remind the reader that it was in Shuja's time that Warren Hastings supplied the services of the British Brigade by whose aid Rohilkund was added to the Province of Oudh. At the accession of Asaf the dominion of the Nawábs extended from the Hills of Kumaon to the Fort of Kalpi; and from Anupshahr above Meerut to the borders of Dahar.

Ásaf-ud-Daulah, though still nominally a Minister and Provincial Governor, assumed the administration of Oudh, with these extended limits, as a feudatory Prince with virtual independence. But his whole principality, with a revenue of more than two and a half millions, was really the fruit of British friendship; since the original part had been settled upon his father by the treaty of Buxar, and the recent additions had been acquired by the aid of the Company's army. Having quarrelled with his mother, he finally abandoned Faizabad and fixed his capital at Lucknow, which he greatly enlarged and beautified. In the great famine of 1784-5, he built the vast halls and mosque in the fort; and on his death in 1798 left a lively memory for largess and liberality.

On Ásaf's death occurred a struggle for the succession, which was claimed by his putative son Wazir Ali; and he actually enjoyed the dignity of Nawáb for a few weeks. But one of the Ministers named Tafazul Hosen, who had been the tutor of a half-brother of the late Ruler, persuaded Sir John Shore, the British Governor-General, that Wazir was not only not the heir, but was personally unfit to govern. The consequence was that Shore went in person to Lucknow and seated the Minister's protegé on the *musnud* by the title of Saádat Ali (II.) deporting the *de facto* Ruler to Benares, where he revenged himself by murdering the Chief Civil Officer, Mr. Cherry.

Saádat Ali further embellished the city and suburbs; and

proved a thrifty and prudent administrator. Lands yielding over a million and a quarter sterling he ceded to the British, by the so called "treaty" of 10th September 1801; but he saw the wisdom of submitting to the will of his foreign masters; and, with their assistance, greatly enhanced the productiveness of the half that was left him, corresponding to the Province as it now exists. Among his other buildings was the once magnificent "Residency;" he also built the house now occupied by the Chief Commissioner, then called, in imitation of a part of the palace at Dehli, the "*Háyát Baksh.*"

From this time the political occupation of the Rulers of Oudh was gone, and they turned their attention to cock-fighting and beast fighting; to fireworks, dancing-girls, and champagne; and they spent the money in the enjoyment of which their powerful protectors guaranteed them in building seraglios and in furnishing them with lustres and mirrors, with glass lions and porcelain negroes.

Saádat Ali died in July 1816, and was succeeded by his eldest son, who took the title of Ghází-ud-Din Haidar; and three years later, on the encouragement of the British Government, openly declared himself an independent King or Emperor. Lord Hastings appears to have thought that by this device he would secure a counterpoise to the Great Moghul; but the people of India never recognized the new royalty: and when the final rally of fifty-seven took place, the Courts of Oudh and Dehli were found to be in the most friendly understanding and co-operation. To those of the native community who interested themselves in politics at all, a Nawáb was still but a Minister, whatever foreigners might call him; and Delhi was still the seat of paramount authority.

Nasir-ud-Din Haidar, son of Ghází, succeeded his father in 1827, and at once plunged into the lowest society, English, Eurasian, and Asiatic. Bred in a purple stye, protected by irresistible allies, his whole reign was one continued satire upon the policy in which it originated. For a notion of the manners of those times the reader may be referred to a book published in London many years ago, called *Private Life of an Eastern*

King. Colonel Low, the Resident, had almost to cease to see the "King," or transact business with him; and Lord W. Bentinck had to hold out strong threats of "direct assumption of the management of the Oude territories by the British Government." Fifteen millions of money left in the "Reserve Treasury" by the frugal Saádat Ali (II.) had now disappeared; and the private profligacy of the present titular absorbed every fraction that could be wrung from the people. Matters were fast reaching a crisis when the dissolute "King" met his death from domestic treachery in July 1837.

A stormy scene ensued. Colonel Low was informed that the *Badshah Begum*, or Queen Dowager, was advancing on the palace with the avowed intention of making King a boy named Munnah Ján, whom she maintained to be the son and heir of the late King then in the Farhat Baksh, and at once sent across the river to Marriaon, where the troops were then cantoned, for a strong detachment of British sepoys. In the meanwhile the old Queen reached the *Lal Báradari*, which stands close in the rear of the Chattan Manjul, and which may be called the "Westminster Hall" of Lucknow. Here she placed the boy on the throne, and vainly sought to intimidate the Resident into making him the customary offering. As in the former case of Wazir Ali, the British were persuaded whether rightly or not that the boy was not really the son of his putative father, and were resolved to elevate a collateral. Whatever may be thought of this policy, there can be but one opinion of the gallantry with which it was carried out. Low resisted all attempts, despite the threats and insults of an infuriated mob; and finally succeeded in joining his own people. A quarter of an hour's grace having expired, a shower of grape-shot was poured upon the building; the sepoys (the 35th N. I., afterwards "the Illustrious" defenders of Jalalabad) charged up the Hall with fixed bayonets; the mob dispersed with severe loss; and by 10 in the morning Mahomed Ali, uncle to the late King, had been proclaimed and crowned. His "reign"—if so it must be called—is noticeable for two things. The last of the Oudh "treaties" was then made, of which the two prominent features were the levying of an auxiliary Brigade paid for by Oudh, and a provision for the partial introduction of British civil administrators. Secondly, no seraglios were built; the only expensive undertaking being the great mosque that lies beyond the Hosenabad Imambára, and is externally at least the handsomest building in Lucknow.

Amjad Ali succeeded peacefully in May 1842, his tenure is chiefly remarkable for the completion of the iron-bridge over the Gumti.

The last King Wájid Âli began to reign in 1847. He was another of the expensive builders; and to him is due the enormous pile of the Kaisar Bágh, on which he is said to have laid out money to the amount of a million sterling. Meanwhile Colonel Sleeman was sent by Lord Dalhousie to examine the state of the country: and the result of his tour, subsequently published in two small octavo volumes, was to make out a strong case for the introduction of direct British management. Contrary, however, to his wishes and advice, the measure in Lord Dalhousie's hands assumed the form of absolute annexation. The feeble voluptuary, who was the nominal Ruler, was removed to Calcutta in 1856, and his removal was speedily followed by the awful explosion to which it probably applied the necessary spark of fire, with one exception the whole intercourse of the late E. I. Company and its officers with Oudh must be confessed to have been tainted, from first to last, by a spirit of rapacity; and all that the Nawábs gained by their consistent fidelity was the privilege of Ontis in the cave of the Cyclops, to be swallowed the last. On the other side are to be set the noble personal qualities that the connexion developed from time to time among the subordinate officials of the Indian Government; the intelligent and sympathetic policy of Lord Canning, the first Viceroy of British India; and the cessation of profligate and selfish expenditure. It must also be admitted that the country has ultimately gained a purer and more prosperous administration without the slightest addition to the burdens of its inhabitants.

The exception to the conduct of the E. I. Company and its

servants above-noted is the case of Lord W. Bentinck, who, in 1831, while fully recognizing the impossibility of a permanent maintenance of the then existing conditions of protected mal-administration, warned the Court of Directors against adding to their own territory, or benefiting their own Exchequer at the expense of Oudh. Unhappily this wise and honorable statemanship met with no appreciation in Leadenhall Street.

Lord William's exact words are the best exponents of his upright and manly policy:—

"Acting in the character of guardian and trustee, we ought to frame an administration entirely native; an administration so composed as to individuals, and so established upon the best principles, revenue and judicial, as should best serve for immediate improvement, and as a model for future imitation. The only European part of it should be the functionary by whom it should be superintended; and it should only be retained till a complete reform might be brought about and a guarantee for its continuance obtained, either in the improved character of the reigning Prince, or, if [he proved] incorrigible, in the substitution of his immediate heir . . . the whole of the revenue being paid into the Oudh Treasury."

A treaty incorporating this principle was executed between the Governor-General and the Nawáb, or King Mahomed Āli, in 1837; but the Court of Directors, disapproving of some details regarding the auxiliary force, did not confirm it, and it was ignored at the annexation—one of their last political acts.

The relevant portions of the text of this treaty, and of that of 1801 to which it refers, will be found in the Appendix.

GENERAL DESCRIPTION OF LUCKNOW.

The visitor will probably arrive at Lucknow from Cawnpore by the Oudh and Rohilkund Railway. It may be also approached by the same line, from Benares and Faizábád, or from Aligurh *viâ* Bareilly. Of the Railways belonging to this Company, it is only necessary to say that their traffic is divided into two classes, the "upper" and "lower," of which the former is very comfortable, each carriage forming a small chamber, fitted up with every requisite, and provided with a bath-room. The speed (or rather the want of speed) may be found somewhat distressing; but it is probable that it is sufficient for the purposes of the country. The Railway-station of Lucknow is near Nasir-ud-Din's Canal; and any number of hackney carriages will be found in front ready to take the traveller in whatever directions he may desire.

Fronting him is the Cawnpore road, leading to the heart of what has been called "The Court Suburb." At the end of this road will be found the *Kaisar Bágh*, and in the neighbourhood a good hotel. To the left are the residency and native city; to the right is the European quarter, Military and Civil, in which there is another hotel, belonging to a native; and farther to the eastward the *Alam Bágh* and other buildings, parks, and gardens.

We will however suppose the traveller to proceed in the direction of the *Kaisar Bágh* and the first mentioned hotel. It is kept at present by Mr. and Mrs. Hill, on some very extensive premises formerly built by Nasir-ud-Din Haidar for the son of his Prime Minister Roshan-ud-Daulah, who was Commander-in-Chief of his Majesty's army. The situation is central, and will admit of a pause from which to study the map, and observe the general features of the whole place.

Lucknow is situated on the banks of the Gumti, a river that takes its rise in some rice-fields in the district of Shahjehanpur in Rohilkund, and which falls into the Ganges beyond Jampur. It is, for the greater part of its course, navigable nearly throughout the year. The city is about 360 feet above sea-level; the latitude being 26°52′ north and longitude 81° east from Greenwich. It extends over about 13 square miles, and contains a population of about 273,126, of whom fifty-nine per cent. are Hindus, and the remaining forty-one Mahomedans, chiefly of the Shia or *Imamia* sect, professed in Persia. There are three roads running south and south-west from the river, the "Outram," the "Aminabad," and the "Canning" roads; the city and cantonments are connected by the strand or road along the river bank, by "Banks" road, and by the "Cantonment-road." The cantonments are separated from the civil lines and city by the disused canal, and cover an area slightly less than that of the city.

Whoever first chose the plain about Lucknow as a site for a great city made an excellent selection.

It stands on and about a rising ground on the right bank of the south of the Gumti, with an inconsiderable suburb and some gardens on the opposite shore. The sites of sixty four ancient townships are said to have been absorbed in the modern city and environs; and the names of many of these are traceable in the names of existing *mohallas* or wards. The original citadel forms the nucleus of the present *Machi Bhawan* Fort, and commands the approach to the so-called "stone-bridge." This eminence, though now crowned by a Moslem mosque, still bears the old Hindu title of *Luchman Tila*, "Luchman Hill;" and, whoever Luchman was, it is thought that his name was the origin of that of Lucknow. As might be expected, the Hindu tradition asserts that the place was founded by the brother of Ráma, whose name was Lachman (more correctly "Laksmana"); and the story goes that his royal brother, after his restoration to the throne of Faizábád, bestowed on him the neighbouring tract of country as a fief. Lachman was attracted to choose this site for his capital—so we are told—by the proximity of the famous World-snake *Sahesnág* (the same whose head was pierced by the rod or pillar near the *Kutb* at Dehli); *Sahesnág*, in those early days (before settling at the Kutb), had taken up his abode on this hillock, and had opened a window in the ground through which he received the sacrificial offerings of his numerous admirers. In other words, the early owners of the place were probably Nágas, with whom the Chatris and Brahmins from Ajudhia contracted an alliance. This ancient landmark, however, has long since disappeared, having been removed by Aurungzeb and replaced by the mosque above referred to.

The Brahmin and other Hindu settlers continued to possess the place until the first Mahomedan conquests. They were then subjugated by one Sayad Salar, a kinsman of Mahmud of Ghazni, about A.D. 1160, and their place as the leading tribe was taken by his followers—a tribe of Shekhs known in later times as the Shahzádas of Lucknow, whose quarters extended from the east of the spot where the *Gol Darwáza* now stands up the walls of the "Residency." All this old city gave great trouble during the mutinies, and has been since levelled, and the site laid out in market gardens. As above indicated the modern Lucknow is of a three-fold character. There is the native town, extensive and populous, consisting of narrow and not over-clean streets and lanes. This is said to have been a foundation of the great Emperor Akbar about the middle of the 16th century A.D. Next comes the court suburb, originating with Asaf-ud-Daulah about a hundred years ago. And lastly to the north and west are the country-houses of the king and his family, the residences of the chief English officials, and the cantonments of the troops.

The first, or purely native commercial quarter, affords but little temptation to the visitor. Entering the arched gateway already mentioned as the *Gol Darwáza*, the pedestrian (for carriages cannot pass) will find himself in a busy-crowded thoroughfare. Here is a line of shops for gold and silver-lace for caps and for other articles of embroidery; there is a banker's and money changer's; there, further on, sits a worker in silver and gilt-chasing, whose particular craft is mainly followed at Lucknow. At the further end of the street, which runs nearly north and south for about a mile, wlll be found a plain archway, called *Akbari Darwáza*, and supposed to have been built by the great Ruler who, as above noted, is said to have founded this part of the place.

Its spandrels are now filled up with the armorial Fish of the Nawábs, but this may possibly be a later addition.

As for the court-suburb in general, the best that can be said for it is that it ought to be seen before Agra and Dehli, or the great ruins of the Deccan cities. Hindustani architecture, when it was built, had fallen into a deep decline; the Hindu artizan, with his patient labor and quaint hereditary fancies, had been neglected or cashiered; stone not being easily available, brick and stucco had to be used; ill-educated Europeans were at hand to give the last finish of vulgarity to design and execution. Nevertheless, it must be added that the vast size of these structures, even their very multitude, tend to create an idea of sumptuousness that is impressive, however tainted with profligate egotism. And the attempt to blend western details with oriental purposes, if not always happily carried out, is at all events capable of producing an occasional effect that is suggestive and not without a grotesque grace. Instances will be found noted below.

Of the European part nothing but praise is to be spoken. The roads are broad, and turf and trees abound. Several beautiful grounds and gardens have been newly laid out or maintained from the past; many of the private residences are handsome and well situated; and the shops and places of business in the *Hazrat Ganj* are unusually handsome. For the intelligent traveller however—especially if of British blood—the main interest of Lucknow must ever be derived from the history of the heroes of Fifty-seven whose remains lie buried there, and of their no less gallant comrades. As Cawnpore is the saddest memorial of British India, so is Lucknow her most glorious. Not even the marvellous campaigns of Lake and Clive, the march of Pollock upon Cabul, or the taking of Dehli by Wilson, can surpass the prowess of their deeds; the first and second defences of the Residency, the desperate attempt at relief by Outram and Havelock, the successful rescue and skilful evacuation under Sir Colin Campbell.

Of the cantonments no more need be said than that they occupy a space of about three miles by four to the south-east of the Railway; the Infantry coming first, then the Artillery, and lastly the Cavalry. There is a large force altogether, and the garrison (of which at least one half is British) forms the head-quarters of a Division. Before the mutiny the bulk of the force was native; and the cantonment was on the left bank of the Gumti.

Every trace of this has disappeared, so rapidly do man and Nature do their work in such a country.

From this general sketch it will be seen that, even more than Calcutta, Lucknow deserves the title of a "City of Palaces." The following picture of its appearance before the annexation may be found interesting :—

"The modern city consists of broad and airy streets, containing the royal palaces and gardens, the principal Musulman religious buildings, the British Residency, and the houses of the various English officers connected with the Court. This part of Lucknow is both curious and splendid, and altogether unlike the other great towns of India, whether Hindu or Mahomedan. There is a strange dash of European architecture among its Oriental buildings. Travellers have compared the place to Moscow and to Constantinople, and can easily fancy the resemblance. Gilded domes surmounted by the crescent ; tall, slender columns ; lofty arcades ; houses that look as if they had been transplanted from Regent Street ; iron railings and balustrades ; cages, some containing wild beasts, others strange bright birds ; gardens, fountains, and cypress-trees ; elephants, camels, and horses ; gilt litters and English barouches ; all these form a dazzling picture."—(*Cal. Rev., Vol. III., p.* 380.)

BRIDGES.

The river, as it passes by, is spanned by four bridges, which (as remarked by a former writer) "serve, in a manner, to indicate in chronological order, through a period of nearly a century, the gradual extension of an originally obscure" town.

The so-called "Stone bridge" is a substantial structure of thirteen pointed arches, that in the centre being much the largest. It is a brick-building erected in the Nawábship of Asaf-ud-Daulah about A.D. 1780. The hog-backed gradient and the variety of the arches give this bridge a quaint and picturesque appearance.

The "Iron bridge" is a very handsome work, the materials of which were sent out from England in 1816 to the order of Ghazi-ud-Din Haidar; but he died before it was erected; and his successors could not be got to take any interest in his project. After the lapse of about thirty years, it was at length put together in the time of Mahomed Ali. His successor completed and opened it, and it now forms a very conspicuous feature in the urban landscape. It consists of three bold segmental arches, supported on arcaded girders; an iron parapet guards the roadway; which is further bordered by lamp-posts and seats for the repose of passengers.

"Bruce's Bridge," so called from the name of the Engineer who constructed it, was put up in 1866; it is of masonry, and like that last described spans the stream with three segmental arches. From this bridge is to be obtained a fine view of the city, imbedded in trees. Looking up the river one sees the old "Stone-bridge;" to the left appear the walls of the *Machi Bhawán* Fort and the great *Imambára.* Further off is seen the lesser *Imambára* backed by the lofty and well proportioned towers of the *Jáma Masjid;* and nearer again, the leafy and picturesque ruins of the "Residency" with its memorial cross in honor of the heroic garrison of 1857. In front are the quaint "umbrella" cupolas of the *Chattar Manzil,* and, at a little distance towards the east, the high domes of the mausoleums that flank the Kaisar Bágh.

Lower down the river is a recent bridge on piles, connecting the *Sikandar Bágh* by way of "Outram Road" with the storehouses of the Commissariat.

In addition to these there is a fifth bridge, still lower down, by which the Railway passes nearly midway between the Martiniere and *Dil Kusha.*

Lastly may be mentioned an unfinished masonry-bridge opposite the Fort, said to have been originally designed by Safdar Jang, son of the founder of the dynasty. The design was abandoned during his life-time, and that of the "Stone-bridge" substituted on the suggestion of his Minister Newal Rai.

Since the annexation many improvements have been introduced, the more interesting of the monuments having been cleaned and repaired, and the city placed under the charge of a municipal board, by whom new bazars have been opened, and order and sanitation everywhere introduced.

Following the natural succession of places as approached from Cawnpore, then, we may first notice the Alam Bágh and Tomb of Havelock. It does not, of course, follow that the new-comer will necessarily find it most convenient to make these the beginning of his inspections.

ALAM BAGH.

This was an enclosure containing a large pavilion and out-offices intended by the ex-king Wajid Ali as an occasional residence for a favourite wife. The architecture is plain and serviceable; but the place derives its chief interest from the part it played in the various relief operations of Havelock, Outram, and Sir Colin Campbell in 1857. During the investment of the Residency, in the summer of that eventful year, the enclosure was strongly held by the rebels; but it was reduced by Havelock, on his advance from Cawnpore, 23rd September. It then became a sort of convalescent depôt, and a basis for further operations. During the subsequent campaign in November the *Bágh* was again utilised. Here the remains of Havelock were interred on the 24th of that month; and during the three succeeding months, when it was found necessary to evacuate Lucknow, Sir James Outram remained here with a small but compact force of all arms as a corps of observation. They were about three thousand strong, attacked and all but invested by a force ten times their strength. But they held their own bravely, and were rewarded by being enabled to greet and join the army advancing to the ultimate reduction on the 1st March 1858. Amongst other famous soldiers, whose names are connected with this enclosure, that of the gallant Outram should never be omitted from honorable mention; though it is byaccident connected in most minds rather with that of Havelock.

Sir H. Havelock, as one learns from the inscription upon his monument, died of dysentery at the *Dil Kusha.* He entered the army in 1815; but, being unable to purchase and not possessed of family influence, he long remained unnoticed and subordinate. In the beginning of 1857 he commanded a Division in Persia, and came round at the termination of the little campaign there just too late to relieve Cawnpore, from whence he accompanied Outram in the first advance on Lucknow. The tenacity of his troops and the chivalry of his brave and unselfish companion are matter of history.

There is nothing of interest to detain the visitor in this quarter. The ruined Fort of Jalalabad, which was the first point seized by Sir Colin in his November advance, is believed to have been built by Shujá-ud-Daulah in 1764 as a defensive post against a possible attack by the British from the eastward. Farther to the eastward are the ruins of Bibiapur, an old park and palace chiefly memorable for having been occupied by Sir John Shore when deposing Wazir Ali and installing Saádat Ali (II). It must have been a plain useful house of the old "Chowringhee" type, but is now unoccupied and falling into decay. The *Walaiti Bágh*, adjoining, is still less important, and only noticeable for its capabilities as a riverside pleasure-ground for whose maintenance there is no provision under a utilitarian Government.

DIL KUSHA.

Free from exaggeration and evidently adapted to the purposes of a country residence, the Dil Kusha was one of the most satisfactory buildings in and about Lucknow. It was built in the early part of the century by Nawáb Saádat (II), and stood in an extensive deer park. But of late years the timber has been removed by some one, and the masonry has accordingly crumbled; in a few years there will be nothing but shapeless ruins to mark the site of what was once a handsome and commodious villa. During the troubles of 1857 this building played an important part. Held in force during the investment of the Residency, it was abandoned by the enemy in November after a running fight of two hours; being attacked and carried by a corps of detachments under Colonel Hamilton of the 78th and occupied as a protection to Sir Colin Campbell's circuitous advance of the 14th and 17th November. At the end of the same month the rescued garrison were brought out of the Residency, and the ladies and the sick accomodated in its walls, on their way to Cawnpore *viâ* the *Alam Bágh;* and here, on the 24th, General Havelock expired of dysentery and weakness, but not before he had heard of the recognition of his services by his Queen and country. A small garden is kept up *taut bien que mal*, at an extravagant expense; otherwise the estate seems strangely neglected and thrown away. It was used as a residence for the general commanding the Division for several years after the mutinies; and it seems a pity that it is not restored to some such use once more.

MARTINIERE.

Turning to the north-west one presently comes upon the house built by General Claude Martine, a native of Lyons, who, after a long career of Eastern adventure, died at Lucknow in 1800 A.D. He left a most curious will, which furnished food for considerable doubt and litigation, in the course of which Lord Brougham delivered a judgment which contains the best attempt in existence to lay down the legal position of the Company and its government in India.

Of the early part of Martine's career not much is known in detail. He appears to have been one of the soldiery of Lally in the struggle made by that rash and unfortunate commander in the Southern Presidency. After the supremacy of the British Rulers of Madras had been completely established, some of these men were formed into a company of Chasseurs under Law, and garrisoned Chandernagore till it was taken by Clive in 1757. It is probable that Martine was one of this small force, and that he then entered the British army, in which he attained the rank of Captain. In 1774 he was employed to survey the boundaries of some of the lands made over about that time to Shuja-ad-Daulah by the British; and he thus came in contact with the Rulers of Oudh. A year or two later he entered their service, with the permission of his own employers, giving up his pay, but retaining his rank and promotion. He now speedily turned his attention to commercial and agricultural pursuits, in which he was for a time associated with the celebrated Count de Boigne. De Boigne had originally become acquainted with Martine in 1783, at the outset of the latter's civil activity, and a friendship had at once sprung up between these two energetic exiles. In 1788, when Sindhia fancied himself able to dispense with the Count's services, they met again; and de Boigne by Martine's advice, invested a considerable sum in the cultivation and manufacture of indigo, afterwards to become such an important part of Indian commerce and even of Indian politics. De Boigne soon renewed his military pursuits, and Martine went on accumulating wealth by himself.

The translator of the *Siyar-al-Motakarin* (Calcutta, 1789) says:—"Col. Martin is a man desirous of all kinds of knowledge; and, although he is at the head of a large fortune which he owes only to his industry, he works whole days together at all the arts that concern watch-making and gunsmith's work with as much bodily labor as if he had his bread to earn by it. As an architect (and he is everything) he has built himself at Lucknow a strong elegant house." It is said that among the accomplishments of this versatile veteran was cock-fighting; he appears in the picture in the Najuf Ashraf, attributed to Zoffany, which represents a main of cocks being fought between the then Resident and the Nawáb Asaf-ud-Daulah. He also managed the mint, gun-foundry, and indigo factory of the same potentate.*

* For a history of the Martiniere School, *vide* Appendix B.

Among other palaces that Martine built was the Farhat Baksh (in which he died), as well as the mansion of Constantia, that we are now examining. In 1800, having attained the rank of Major-General in the Company's service, Martine died, leaving a fortune estimated at over four hundred thousand pounds, of which about three-fourths were bequeathed to the three cities of Lucknow, Lyons, and Calcutta, for the foundation of schools in each.

It is said that the Nawáb Asaf-ud-Daulah was so pleased with this Constantia-House when it was completed, that he offered to buy it for a crore of rupees (a million sterling). But the General, having destined it for other uses, did not accept the offer; and the only effect of it was to suggest to his mind a singular expedient to prevent the property from being so seized after his death. A Musulman Ruler might violate the right of property, he might tear up a testament, or frustrate charitable intentions, but he would probably respect a tomb. With keen perception of this feature of Oriental character, the General bequeathed the house to the school, and ordered that his remains should be interred in one of the apartments. The sepulchre was accordingly constructed, and the body laid in a vaulted chamber of the basement; but the rebels of 1857 dug up the place in search of treasure, and, in their disappointment at not finding any, scattered the bones about the place. It is understood that they have since been restored to their original receptacle, which is a plain sarcophagus resting on the floor.

The building consists of a well-raised basement-storey, with extensive wings and a *bizarre* superstructure, chiefly remarkable for the superposition of one of the Grecian orders upon another, and the abundance of statues in brick-work and plaster; the small pavilions that break the sky-line; the crenellations varied by figures of lions standing erect, holding on to the battlements with one paw, while they gesticulate oratorically, with the other, make up an ensemble which is certainly unique, and may even be called "striking." High over all rises the central tower crowned with a *belvedere* and flag-staff supported by flying buttresses, and affording a wide prospect.

The main building is devoted to the use of a school containing nearly two hundred boys, with the necessary halls and dormitories, to which has been recently added a chapel formed in the central room. Of the wings one contains class-rooms, the other the refectory.

In front is a dreary sheet of water chiefly used for the washing of clothing. There is a small mound in it, supporting a strange isolated Ionic column, of which the entablature has only part of a capital and supports an octagonal pavilion topped by a little cupola serving no apparent purpose. There is a large garden surrounded with plantations, and on one side of the road leading to the west is a monument to the gallant William Hodson, who died in the *Háyát Baksh*, now the residence of the Chief Commissioner.

WINGFIELD PARK.

Crossing the canal and turning to the right, one comes to the Wingfield Park, a handsome garden of about 40 acres, which owes much of its beauty to the taste and skill of Dr. Bonavia. It occupies the site of an old native enclosure called the *Banárasi Bágh*, or "Benares Garden," and derives its present name from a former Chief Commissioner—now Sir Charles Wingfield, M.P.—who caused it to be laid out in its present form. The turf, trees, and roads are finely varied, and the small space utilised to the utmost extent. Its flowers, especially its roses, are among the finest in Upper India; it is however a question whether it would not be sufficiently availed of as a mere *Jardin d' Acclimation*, and the pleasure-ground and driving-space extended towards the north in the direction of the river. In the central part of the "Park" is a beautiful pavilion, or Báradari, in the Moghul style of architecture, which once formed a prominent ornament of the *Hazrat Bágh* in the precincts of the *Kaisar Bágh*, or palace of Wájid Ali. It was removed from thence and reconstructed in its present situation; the jewelled inlay, which had suffered in the disturbances, being repaired with coloured mastic, or some other inexpensive substitute. In this building the residents of Lucknow hold flower-shows and festive meetings, and the floor is said to be a good one for dancing.

The park was laid out by Mr. Reginald Berkeley, Assistant Commissioner, whose plans were afterwards modified by Messrs. Morrison and Hodges, acting under directions from Sir C. Wingfield and General Barrow. It is unfortunate that provision for its due maintenance was not at the same time made; the seven hundred pounds now available from local funds being barely adequate to the small area now kept up, and wholly insufficient for an extension, even on the most unambitious scale.

SIKANDAR BAGH.

Due north of the Wingfield Park will be found the somewhat fantastic gateway of a large walled enclosure called *Sikandar Bágh*, after Sikandar Begum, one of the Sultáness of the ex-King for whom it was constructed. To the right of the gate is a place where the wall was breached during the advance of Sir Colin Campbell, on the 16th November 1857. When—as was at that time the case—the walls were complete and loopholed for musketry, it formed a strong fortification against everything but artillery; and it was desperately defended by a body of more than 2,000 rebels, all trained soldiers of the revolted Bengal army. The 93rd Highlanders, with some detachments of British and Sikh Infantry, entered by the breach and bayonetted the whole of the defenders. The walls are now dilapidated, and there is nothing in the place to detain the traveller. The ground might be included in a "People's Park," the gateway being, of course, preserved.

KADAM RASUL AND SHAH NAJAF.

A little to the west will be observed a mound overhanging the river, and embowered in thickets of bamboo and other vegetation.

It is a plain building, of the usual tomb-character, surmounted by a well-proportioned dome flanked by small pinnacles; and is called *Kadam Rasul*, or "Apostle's Step," from being supposed to contain a stone marked with the footprint of the founder of Islam, brought from Mecca. It was built by the first "King" of Oudh, Ghazi-ud-Din Haidar. The present existence of the stone however is doubtful. This commanding point was also held by the rebels, who endeavoured to oppose Genl. Campbell; but it was captured without much difficulty. In the same direction is the *Najaf Ashraf*, known in Histories of the War as the "Shah Najeef." It contains the sepulchre of the King just mentioned, who built it with the intention that it should be so employed: and the name—"Reverend Najaf" is derived from that of the tomb of Ali, the son-in-law of Mahomed, and chief patriarch of the Shias, of which it purports to be a copy: the dome is flat without being structurally correct; and the style of the architecture generally unsatisfactory. Being surrounded with a high wall, it formed a prominent part of the enemy's defences on the occasion above referred to; but it was taken by storm by the sailors of the *Shannon*, let by their heroic Captain William Peel, and supported by a small body of Infantry. It contained a fine marble pavement, and many decorations in glass, which were all destroyed or greatly injured by the Tars, but have been since to some extent restored. It also contains some curious pictures, probably the work of Zoffany. It is maintained by an endowment founded by Ghazi-ud-Din, and is illuminated twice a year, once at the *Moharam*, and once on the anniversary of the Founder's death, on which occasions great crowds are always assembled. It is a curious trait of past times, and one which tends to exhibit the confidence formerly felt in the stability and integrity of the British Government, that the funds for these entertainments, and for the general maintenance of the building and of its establishment, were provided by the loan of a crore of rupees (about one million sterling) to the East India Company. The Governor-General, Lord Amherst, on the Company's behalf, undertook, in consideration of the payment of this sum, to guarantee in perpetuity the disbursement of Rs. 41,666, being the interest thereof at five per cent. per annum. Out of this, monthly payment Rs. 1,137 were to be paid to the persons attached to the *Najaf Ashraf* (then styled "the new Imambára"), and the balance to the wives, sons, daughters, and other dependents of the King, with remainder to this foundation and that of the Karbala, to be hereafter described, in the event of any of them dying childless and intestate.—*(Agreement of 30th September* 1825.*)*

MOTI MAHAL.

Still going west, and keeping close to the line of Sir Colin's attack, we reach the "Pearl-Palace," said to have been so called from the shape of a structure on the roof, which no longer exists. It was part of a series of river-side pleasure-houses built by the Nawab Saádat Ali (II) in the beginning of the century, in whose courtyards the ram-fighting and similar sports in vogue at the courts of Native Chiefs used to take place. Like so many buildings in the neighbourhood, the Moti Mahal was fortified in 1857, and was stormed, after an hour's fighting, on the 17th November. The enemy took one of Sir Colin's guns for a time, but it was recovered by the gallantry of Lieut. Crump, of the Madras Artillery, who received his death-wound in bringing off the piece, but effected his object with the aid of Private Duffy, of Her Majesty's 90th Foot, who fortunately survived to receive the Victoria Cross. Col. Lewis Cooper, R. A., the Brigadier in command, was killed in the courtyard of the Moti Mahal, as was also Dr. Bartram; Col. Campbell of the 90th here received his death-wound. It has since been purchased from Government by the Maharájah of Balrámpur.

KHURSHED MANZAL.

Over the way is a plain substantial house, which was also strongly fortified and held by the enemy; but has been converted since to the peaceful uses of a girls' school attached to the

Martiniere foundation. The storming-party consisted of detachments of the 53rd and 90th Foot, augmented by the famous "naval brigade" with their heavy guns, and supported by some Sikh Infantry. It is the "Belle Alliance" of Lucknow, being the point whither Outram and Havelock came from the relieved Baillie-guard to greet their deliverer Sir Colin Campbell. In the short run from the Residency these Generals lost nearly half their party from the enfilading fire of which they had to run the gauntlet. "The scarped ditch is now a bright green lawn for the children's play-ground, and the towers make airy bedrooms for the little girls." This school, though now affiliated to the Martiniere, formed no part of the Founder's original purpose, having been developed out of the trust by the thoughtfulness and benevolence of General and Mrs. Saunders Abbott, and finally started on its existing basis and scale in 1869.

The next link in the chain of rebel-fastnesses was the *Tára Koti*, or "Star House," originally built for an observatory by the second King Nasir-ud-Din Haidar. The walls were demolished after the mutiny, and the building modernised and converted into the office of the Bank of Bengal. On the south is an open space; and close by on the right hand, a curiously shaped monument of "gothic" character commemorates the spot where Sir Mountstuart Jackson, Bart, C.S., and a party of ladies and gentlemen who were shot on the 24th September 1857, after being captured in concealment in the city. The head of the party that murdered them, Rajah Jailal Singh, was subsequently executed, and his property forfeited to the State.

Several fine houses are to be seen in this neighbourhood; but as they have been completely Europeanised, and are in the occupation of private families, it is unnecessary to confuse the traveller with a description of what they were or are now.

All were included in the lines of defence adopted by the enemy in 1857-8, and all were carried in the same undaunted way on two, or even three, occasions. The demolition of the walls has completely destroyed the identity of these buildings and enclosures. The visitor leaving them to his right, will next come upon the Palaces of the last King of Oudh, Wájid Ali Shah.

KAISAR BAGH.

This great group was begun in A.D. 1848, and finished in 1850, and is admitted to have cost a million of money. It is difficult to say how much of the labor was compulsory and unremunerated; on the other hand the peculation of clerks and other higher employés was probably unchecked and enormous. The result was an immense courtyard with fantastic buildings on all four sides; a stucco Louvre, in which Italian and Moorish styles blend in a manner that is more grotesque than graceful; and where gilding, and ochre, and whitewash tend to give a strange appearance of the theatre to the "residency" of this Oriental Gerolstein. It thus furnishes fair occasion for political moralising; and better represents the histrionic majesty produced by one viceregal manager, and withdrawn by another than a more sober and substantial structure would have done. It must be added that the architecture denotes a step, since followed out by Messrs. Chisholm, Emerson, and Mant, towards a style in which the germs of a national art are probably to be looked for. And there are portions of the Kaisar Bágh itself—such as the gateway photographed in the *Lucknow Album*—which, as mere outline, are not without dignity. Here, as in so many of the Lucknow monuments, it is not so much the design as the material that is so disappointing and so pregnant with premature decay. And, after all is said, these buildings must be admitted to be quite too good for their purpose, the seclusion of the countless concubines of a puppet, and the lair of his crapulous satiety.

Besides the great quadrangle there were many detached quarters, each with its own garden; while the central space was tastefully laid out, and filled with parterres, lawns, and falling fountains. Statues abounded in the walks, and the chambers glistened with lustres, mirrors, gilt furniture, and woven or embroidered hangings, all of which have perished.

What remains of these splendours has been made over as a sort of caravanserai for the use of the landed aristocracy—the famous talukadars of Oudh. It may be added that the spoliation of the chambers and galleries of this vast range of buildings was due rather to the rebels than to their British conquerors, though the latter very generally administered in the long run. The slaughter here, in Sir Colin's first advance, was very considerable. Havelock's advance in the previous September had also to come this way, and here he suffered severe loss, having had to cross the canal at the Chár Bágh under heavy fire and bear the brunt of all the intervening batteries in a bee-line, up the Cawnpore road and by the *Háyát Bakhsh.* In this desperate struggle the chief brunt was borne by the 78th Highlanders and the Sikh Regiment of Firozpur.

Flanking the entrance of the Kaisar Bágh are two large and handsome sepulchres in the usual Italianised style, but forming exceptionally good specimens. These mark the last resting-place of Saádat Ali, the father, and Morshidzadi, the mother, of Ghazi-ud-Din the first king, by whom they were built. Many of the details are of the Hindustani School; but the dome of the Nawáb's tomb is almost as good as any in Europe; while that of his wife's monument rises out of a peculiar, but very pleasing, group of pillars and arches. These buildings may be cited as favorable examples of the union of European ideas with Asiatic work; and the critical visitor, turning from them to less happy instances around, may be tempted to say "*omnia si sic!*"

KAISAR PASAND.

At the south-west angle of the Kaisar Bágh stands a still more fantastic structure than the great palace itself—with which, however, it tallies well. Ionic columns, balustrades with globe-like finials, Moorish minarets, Hindu umbrellas; arches, pediments, lanterns; are all blended in a confusion which the eye may long seek vainly to disentangle, and surmounted with an unmeaning gilt band.

It was originally built, in the time of the dissolute Nasir-ud-Din Haidar, by his Minister Raushan-ud-Daulah, the father of the Commandar-in-Chief, whose quarters form the present hotel just opposite. It adds much to the horror of the Massacre of Sir M. Jackson, and his party, just described, to know that they had been confined in the cellars of this building for some time before. It is however possible to comfort oneself by reflecting that, perhaps, under the circumstances, death came as a relief. These poor captives may have heard of Havelock's arrival at the Alam Bágh; and, if they were led to believe that his advance would fail, it may well be imagined that life in such captivity had few charms and death no terror.

The Kaisar Pasand had fallen into the possession of the last King Wájid Ali, and was used by him as the residence of a female favourite. Since the mutiny it has been converted to more practical if less romantic uses; "its spacious and lofty rooms" being now appropriated to the Courts, Offices, treasury, and other purposes of the District *Kachehri*.

At the end of the road running west from the Kaisar Bágh is a gate formerly called *Sher Darwáza*, but now consecrated to the memory of the heroic Neil; who marched up with his Madras Fusiliers from Benares to Allahabad, then joined in the too tardy occupation of Cawnpore, and finally fell on this spot, as he was leading his small force to the first place in the relief of the Residency. He was killed by a round-shot from the Kaisar Bágh batteries. His statue, in white marble, surmounts the archway; and the whole forms a very suitable memorial for a gallant soldier.

We are now close to the shores of the winding Gumti, and to Bruce's Bridge, the view from which has been already noticed.

CHATTAR MANZAL.

The most fantastic of all Lucknow's fantastic piles is now before us, the *chattar*, or umbrella, house, so called from the strange gilt ornament which crowns the summit. This was the great *sérail* of the debauched Nasir-ud-Din, by whom it was built; and was originally surrounded by a strong and high brick wall intended to secure the seclusion of its inmates. This circumstance made it a very powerful element in the defence of Lucknow by the rebels; and it was the scene of a severe cannonade during Havelock's advance. The best rooms are now appropriated to the various uses of the United Service Club: the Theatre, and Assembly Rooms; the large and valuable public Library; and other similar purposes. There are numerous detached buildings, built in a purer style, and admirably adapted to the use of the Civil Courts and offices of the Public Works to which they are now for the most part, appropriated.

LALL BÁRADARI.

The most interesting and important of these is the *Lall Báradari*, formerly an annex of the old palace of Farhat Baksh, which is now partly demolished and partly turned into a private residence. The Baradari itself, which was once the Westminster Hall of Oudh, has continued to fill a similar rank ever since the mutinies; seeing that, in the event of a general Durbar, it is still used for the reception of privileged guests. As will be seen it is a very handsome building; suffering, indeed, from the quantity of red ochre which has been smeared over the masonry in a fraudulent endeavour to give it the effect of a red-stone building like those of Agra and Dehli; but possessing some of the dignity of design that stamps most Moghul buildings. The scene that occurred here on the death of Nasir-ud-Din has been already briefly referred to. The paramount power was represented by Col. Low, a gallant and intelligent officer who became subsequently a member of the Government of India. Whether rightly or wrongly, the Resident had become convinced that Munna Jan, the youth whom the Queen Dowager (*Badshah Begum*) was putting forward, was not the son of the late King, and that—by the laws of the Imámia School—the succession devolved upon his uncle, an old and timorous man named Mahomed Ali. On the night of the 7th July news of the King's death was brought to the Residency; upon which Col. Low at once proceeded to *Farhat Bahsh*, a palace near the Chattar Manzal, and sent across the river directions to the Brigadier to call out 1,000 men, and follow them up with the whole remaining infantry and guns of the garrison. The approaches to the *Lall Báradari* were then guarded, as well as the resources available would permit; and at 3 A.M. the new King was brought to the palace where he occupied a room looking down upon the river. Meanwhile the pretender, led by his putative grandmother, advanced upon the *Lál Báradari* with a tumultuous following, and placed himself upon the throne. The Resident immediately proceeded thither, and a scene of great tumult ensued. The four halls, the small apartments, and the verandahs were filled with armed men; swords and spears clashed; blunderbusses were discharged, answered by *salvoes* of artillery from the surrounding streets; while a party of nautch girls whirled before the throne to the accompaniment of wild barbaric music by the light of smoking flambeaux. Imperturbable amid the confusion Colonel Low urged his remonstrances upon the Begum; threatened, hustled, the intrepid officer resisted all attempts to make him do homage to the throne with its usurping occupant. A general outbreak seemed at hand. But a friendly noble contrived at this juncture to lead Low from the hall, and in the garden appeared the welcome spectacle of Brigr. Monteath at the head of five companies of regular troops. Presently they were joined by an emissary of the Begum's, who was informed by the Resident that if the building was not evacuated in a quarter of an hour the troops would proceed to act without farther delay. But the infatuated lady remained firm to her purpose; and, on the expiry of the time of grace, the artillery opened upon the *Lál Báradari* with a discharge of grape shot. After six or seven rounds, a Company of the 35th was directed to storm the building. As they entered the hall at the end opposite the throne, they saw their own figures reflected in a huge mirror behind the throne; and, taking what they saw for an opposing party, they poured their first volley into the looking-glass. This put the mob to flight; the soldiers, charging up the hall with fixed bayonets, drove them out on the north side, and followed them through the adjacent court-yard. In a few minutes the building was cleared off its late tumultuous occupants, with the exception of about fifty, who lay dead or wounded upon the floors. The Begum and her protégé were taken into custody, and sent to the Residency; but it was late in the forenoon before order was completely restored. Search was then made for poor old king, who was found concealed in an apartment of the Palace. Here he was presently soothed and prepared for his enthronement in that hall that had been the scene of so much noise and bloodshed. The ceremony took place under a royal salute from the British artillery, repeated by all the guns in the city saved from massacre and plunder by the firmness of one man. Since that night of terror the *Lál Báradari* has made one more appearance in history, when it witnessed a scene of a quieter, though still more momentous character. It was here that, after the restoration of order, Lord Canning came to meet the Talukadárs of Oudh, and to announce to them the forgiveness of the Queen of Great Britain, and the terms of their future allegiance.

Of the Palace to which this building once formed the *Diwan-i-Am*, or grand entrance hall, little need be said. It has already been mentioned as having been built by General Martine and the place of his death. Subsequently to that event it continued to be the chief dwelling place of the Rulers of Oudh until the completion of the Kaisar Bágh in the time of the last king. It is thus described by Miss Eden, who visited it in company with her brother Lord Auckland, shortly before the events above-recorded:—

"There are four small Palaces, fitted up in the eastern way, with velvet and gold and marble, with arabesque ceilings, orange-trees and roses in all directions . . . . And in one Palace there was an immense bath-room of white marble, the arches intersecting one another . . . and the marble inlaid with cornelian and bloodstone; in every corner . . . there were little fountains; even during the hot winds, they say it is cool from the quantity of water playing."

These buildings were the last captured in Havelock's advance. The enemy however reoccupied them between the 25th September and Campbell's relief; and the batteries placed there had given great trouble till breached and stormed by the crew of the *Shannon*, and the Highland Brigade. The masonry pier in the water marks the spot where the Kings of Oudh had a fishing-pavilion in the middle of the stream. The greater portion of these deserted Palaces were as already stated demolished, and the remains have been converted into private dwellings, together with their dependencies upon the other bank.

RESIDENCY.

We are now at the spot which in all Lucknow possesses the deepest historic interest. Before us is the "Baillie Guard," so called from Colonel Baillie, one of the British Residents in the early part of the century, who built it as an approach, or defence to the Residency. It is but a simple and common place archway, yet one that has undergone almost as much cannonading as many a first-class fortress. It must, of course, be understood that the mouth of the main arch was built up with the strongest rubble; but even so, it seems wonderful that so frail a defence should have proved so useful.

The charming undulating grounds of to-day give but little notion of the space wherein thousands of persons, combatant and non-combatant, male and female, were cooped up and rained upon with shot and shell for fifteen weeks. On the right front stands the ruins of the "Residency," properly so called, a magnificent mansion, built about the end of the last century by the then Nawab Saádat (II) for the use of his foreign bear-leader. the cellars underneath were harboured the women and children of the 32nd Foot; the upper rooms and adjacent banquetting house formed an imperfect shelter for a portion of the officers and staff. To the left front in Dr. Fayrer's house, the ladies lived in the underground rooms, the ground floor being used as a Hospital. Being on high ground the upper parts of the main buildings were soon reduced into the state in which we now behold them; but the watch tower on the top of the Residency was used as a look-out all through the siege; and, even in its present shattered condition, affords one of the best views of the city. In this perilous "crow's nest" an officer was constantly stationed with a field glass to keep watch on the movements of the enemy; and in November Sir James Outram erected a Semaphore there, by means of which he contrived to communicate with Sir Colin at the Alambagh and Dilkusha with a preconcerted code of signals. All these spots are marked with stone tablets; and an excellent further idea may be formed of the relative positions of the various buildings, within and without, by the aid of a model, by the Rev. Mr. Moore, which is in the museum just outside the Baillie Guard.

Beginning, then, with this part, we notice first the Lawrence Memorial, a somewhat peculiar—not to say ungraceful—cross, said to have been designed by an amatuer architect of those days, Mr. C. B. Thornhill. Placed upon the highest part of the grounds it somewhat superfluously commemorates the name of Henry Lawrence, to whom the whole place is a monument, and whose tomb, with its simple epitaph, is in the cemetery adjoining.

To the north stood the "Redan-battery," commanding the passage over the Iron Bridge (already described) and serving as a check upon the enemy's guns planted across the river in the *Búdshah Bágh*. This post was held, throughout the whole siege, by Lieutenant Lawrence, Her Majesty's 32nd Foot. The low land to the northward was the Residency garden in old times. The adjoining cemetery marks the spot where the bodies of the brave men who perished in the defence were laid. The next point of interest is that marked by the foundations of the house occupied by Mr. Martin Gubbins, C.S., which, commanded by Major Ashton, 41st N. I., bravely held out throughout the siege. Adjoining will be found traces of a small swimming-bath, which the doughty Financier had intended to economise for the use of his small garrison, to the strict exclusion of all outsiders. By one of those comic coincidences which will so often be found lighting up the grimmest scenes of human life, this small and apparently sheltered structure was struck by a shell on the very first day of the siege; and, amid loud shouts of laughter from the banished bye-standers "Buggins' Bath," as it had been irreverently denominated, disappeared hopelessly interred in its own ruins. Next to this stood the house of another Civil Servant, Mr. Ommaney, who was unhappily killed there. Next to this was the "Brigade Mess house," of which the traces are still discernible. Here were the head-quarters of the garrison under Colonel John Inglis the Brigadier; and it was ably defended by a party of chosen marksmen, all officers, whose rifles kept up a constant and withering fire upon imprudent rebels exposing themselves to the attentions of the cool intrepid men, trained to field-sports, who never threw a shot away. The "Enfield rifle" had then been newly invented, and a few of these weapons had found their way to Lucknow. These, together with the numerous sporting-rifles in the possession of the officers, formed one of the most terrifying and efficient portions of the defence. A little to the right front was the "Sikh-Square" the scene of one of the most successful of the enemy's mining operations. When it was blown into the air three officers were sent flying into the enemy's entrenchments; but the enemy had retired for the explosion; and the officers, alighting unhurt, coolly returned to the place from whence they came. Less fortunate were some poor drummers, who were buried alive under the ruins of some buildings, and whose screams were heard in the pauses of the cannon, from 9 in the morning till 2 in the afternoon. When at last a party was able to reach the spot and dig them out, death had put a period to their sufferings.

We next reach the terrible "Cawnpore-battery," the perilous guard of this frail fortress. So desperate was this post considered that no officer was placed in permanent charge of it, but it was either held by volunteers, or by men told off from day to day according to the roster. At less than a stone's throw the enemy were posted in a strongly fortified house; and it was not until a mine had been successfully run under it and the whole blown into the air that the defence of this quarter could be considered as anything but most precarious. Here fell the gallant Radcliffe, of the 7th Bengal Cavalry, the dashing officer who, as commandant of the handful of Volunteer Horse, had, by repeated and furious charges, covered the retreat from the disastrous field of Chinahat. Close to this was a post, held bravely throughout the siege by 65 boys from the Martiniere,* who, in addition to military duty, gave general assistance as hospital attendants, signallers, and in a variety of other ways. Many of these noble little fellows grew to manhood, and are now members of the Lucknow Rifle Volunteers.

A little to the rear was a post held by a gallant Frenchman named Duprat, who, resisting all offers from the enemy, cast in his lot with his hereditary rivals, and maintained his post until he met with a soldier's end.

The next post was held by Capt. Anderson, 25th N.I., who afterwards published a vivid narrative of the siege. His post was hardly more tenable than the Cawnpore-battery, and its shelter was completely destroyed before the end of the siege; the commandant and Mr. Capper, C.S., being literally buried in the ruins, but fortunately escaping without serious damage.

Here runs a lane which, only guarded by a feeble traverse, led in the direction of Dr. Fayrer's house. But such was the terror inspired by the courage and skill of the white-faces that the enemy were never able to effect an entrance.

Such was the disposition, and such the nature of the various principal defences of this marvellous siege; necessitated by the annexation of Oudh and by all its fearful consequences, but precipitated, doubtless, by the disaster of Chinahat. The city of Lucknow and its adjoining cantonments had been kept in order up to the end of June by the firm and vigilant measures of Sir H. Lawrence; and this precious interval was made the best use

---

* *Vide* App. D.

of by him in the collections of stores of ammunition and provisions in anticipation of the coming storm. On the 29th June Sir Henry learned that a body of rebels was advancing upon Lucknow, and on the following morning a portion of the garrison, on whom it was thought safe to depend, marched out to meet them. It. consisted of a small body of about 500 infantry, forty mounted volunteers, 120 native troopers, a detail of artillery manned by native gunners, and an 8-inch howitzer drawn by an elephant. To the surprise of the leaders, on arriving on the ground six miles distant, a complete army composed of an overwhelming force of all arms, was found drawn up in order of battle. The native artillerymen deserted their guns; the howitzer had to be abandoned; the small British force was speedily enveloped; Colonel Case of the 32nd and nearly a hundred of his men were killed; and, but for the unwearied efforts of the mounted volunteers and the inconceivable omission on the part of the enemy to hold or destroy the Iron-bridge, not a man would have returned. As it was, out of the small expedition, 172 Europeans were killed or wounded, including 13 military officers—more than half the entire number—and the survivors had only time to blow up the Machi Bhawan Fort when they found themselves strictly invested in the Residency Grounds. The siege thus began on the 1st July: the strength of the garrison consisting of no more than 927 Europeans, and 765 natives, 230 of whom deserted during the succeeding leaguer. On the 4th the chivalrous Lawrence breathed his last, from the effects of a wound in the leg inflicted as he sate writing in the Residency-house, by a fragment of a shell from his own lost howitzer.

Some faint idea of the long days that followed may be derived from *Day by Day in Lucknow.** For further particulars Capt. Anderson's book on the defence of Lucknow—already referred to—may be consulted; as also the work, on the same subject, of the late Mr. Martin Gubbins.

---

* A Diary by Colonel Case's widow.

The nature of the advance of Havelock (under whom Sir James Outram with characteristic generosity placed himself as a simple volunteer, though he was the senior officer) has been partially traced in the description of some of the buildings that he had to pass. By the time that his force entered the side doorway of the Baillie Guard on the 26th September, the strength of the garrison had been reduced to 1179, the loss having been chiefly among the Europeans. Out of 9 officers of the Bengal Artillery 5 had fallen; eleven ladies and 53 children had been slain or had succumbed to their privations and trials; and between that date and the final relief by Sir Colin Campbell on the 17th of the following November, 122 more of the old garrison and 400 of Havelock's men had died. Far from relieving the garrison, this arrival only added to its privations. It does not, however, appear that there was ever any actual failure of the necessaries of life. It should be added that after entering the Residency, Outram assumed command of the final relief led to by the combination of tactics and hard fighting already glanced at: little need be said except that it was one of the most skilful movements ever effected in war. The ladies and non-combatants left on the 19th, and, on the night of the 22nd November, the Residency and its grounds were silently evacuated, and each of the positions held along the road to the *Dilkusha* abandoned in its turn. The long-enduring women were hospitably received at the *Dilkusha* as they arrived; and here the sick were cared for, and here Havelock—his work accomplished—sank under the fatigues he had undergone, leaving Outram to watch the rebels in the *Alum Bágh.* Sir Colin Campbell conducted the precious convey he had done so much to save along the Cawnpore road; and though Cawnpore itself was fiercely threatened, led them across the bridge of boats, and finally forwarded the refugees and treasure in safety to Allahabad, which they reached on the evening of the 7th December.

These are the bare facts; but the most skilful pen would fail to convey any notion of all that they imply. Gazing to-day upon the peaceful garden-scene, one cannot realize the terrors and tumult of those frightful months. One must be content with imagining the roar of artillery and the rattle of small arms kept up incessantly from before sunrise for more than three hours daily by an investing swarm of a hundred thousand relentless savages; the lull of the weary noon-day; the resumption of hostilities in the long afternoon at a season when Europeans in India are wont to shield themselves from the depressing glare or plunging rain, and rest within cool houses; the sallies, the rallies, the mines and countermines; the explosions of roofs, the downward rushes of crumbling masonry; and worst of all the slow decay of wounds and epidemics, sustained in crowded rooms, amid a plague of flies, with insufficient food; finally the incessant monotony of daily funerals. Small-pox was prevalent; women brought forth children only to bury them; Polehampton the chaplain, after being shot through the body, died of cholera, which seems to have been chronic, especially among non-combatants—officers were on several occasions shot by the sentries inadvertently; some few even committed suicide. But despair was the exception; and the general endurance deservedly received the admiration of the world.

BALRAMPUR HOSPITAL.

On the site of some of the houses from which the Residency-garrison was most fiercely pressed on the side of the Cawnpore road, the Rajah of Balrampur has lately caused to be erected a number of plain substantial buildings to serve as a Hospital and Medical School, and has founded an endowment for its maintenance.

MACHI BHAWAN.

Nor far from the Residency is the iron-bridge by which the remains of the ill-fated expedition returned from Chinahat. Keeping along the river a road goes west to the so-called stone-bridge, and on the left will be seen a small mosque upon a rising ground. This is the building raised by the fanatical Emperor Aurangzeb upon the site of the Serpent's home on *Lachman Tila;* and all round are the lines of the *Machi Bhawan*, or "Fish-buildings," said to be so called from the heraldic emblem of Oudh. This is the stronghold that was blown up after the retreat from Chinahat, on which occasion 240 barrels of powder and six million ball-catridges were destroyed. It has now been extended so as to embrace the great *Imámbára*, and will, for the future, take rank as a second class fortress.

GREÂT IMÁMBÁRA.

The exact meaning of the word *Imámbára* is "Patriarch's Place," which is a title given by the Shiah Musalmans of Oudh to a building consecrated to the *Moharam*, or celebration of the martyrdom of the sons of Ali, the immediate descendants of the Prophet, put to death by rival claimants to the headship of Islam in the 40th year of the *Hijra* (666 A.D.). The *Moharam*, a moveable celebration, lasts ten days, and is now shared by all classes of Mohamedans, and even by many of the uneducated classes of Hindus. The ceremonial begins by the exhibition of *Tawdry* frame-works of wood-work and tinsel called *tázias*, supposed to represent the tomb of Hosen at Karbala in Turkish Arabia. These are kept on view for ten days, during which a fast and lamentation are maintained. Upon the 10th day a sort of funeral procession takes place, with crowds of armed men, mourners, etc., accompanied by wild barbaric music, and ending in the symbolical sepulture of the *tázias* in the place appointed for the purpose. The *Imámbáras* are illuminated, and hymns chanted there in honour of the martyrs.

The buildings that we are now considering possess several claims to notice, in their vast size, their striking style, and their origin. In the year 1784 A.D. occurred a great famine, still remembered in the annals of the people as the *Chalisa*, or

"Forty" from the Hindi year, Sambat 1840, in which it happened. On this the Nawáb Asaf-ud-Daulah resolved to commence this work as a measure of the out-door relief; and it is said that upwards of a million sterling was expended before it was completed. Kaifiat Ullah is said to have been the architect whose designs were adopted; and tradition adds that many of the hitherto prosperous citizens were so reduced by want as to be compelled to take up the trowel or the hod among the more experienced masons. In order to spare their sense of shame at this degradation, the Nawáb considerately allowed the wages of these retiring amateurs to be paid at night. So goes the story: About the middle of the central room are interred the remains of the Founder. "The hall was usually illuminated with a profusion of wax tapers and numerous hanging lights, the tomb itself being strewn with flowers, and covered with cakes of barley from Mecca; officiating priests in attendance day and night, chanting verses from the Koran" *(Brown)*. These decorations and uses are alike gone; and the building is now appropriated to military purposes, being an arsenal for the guns and ammunition of the Fort in which it has been included. The dimensions of this hall are 167 feet by 52 feet, and the total height is said to be 63 feet. It may be added that this vast building is a fine specimen of constructive skill, being built throughout of solid masonry unassisted by the use of any timber. It is also remarkable that no permanent provision appears to have been made—as in the case of the *Najaf Ashraf*—for the maintenance of the repairs, the celebrations and the establishment. To the right of the great quadrangle will be observed a mosque with lofty minarets, only inferior to those of the great *Jama Masjid* to be presently noticed. This mosque forms a portion of the original design, and greatly enhances its magnificence.

RÚMI DARWAZA.

Passing on towards the Hosenabad, or Lesser *Imámbára*, the visitor goes through a gate something in the style of an enormous cockle-shell, flanked on either hand by a low curtain wall, topped by small arcades, and ending in octagonal bastions. Like the vast building we have just quitted it is the work of the lavish *Asaf-ud-Daulah*, who lived in the *Daulat Khána*, a ruin in the vicinity, before the *Farhat Baksh* was made into a Palace. The street here is very broad and fine, and leads to the next building.

HOSENABAD.

The Lesser *Imámbára* was the work of the last king but two, Mohamed Ali, whom we have seen installed by Colonel Lowe after the hopeless attempt of Munnah Ján. It was originally endowed with twelve lakhs of rupees, and formed the tomb of its founder, as also a vast repository of mirrors, lustres, etc., the greater part of which still remain. During the disturbances of 1857 it escaped the shocks of war; but the more valuable part of its furniture, the gold and silver plate, was taken away by the trustees themselves, to aid the rebel cause, together with the Government securities which formed the endowment. Duplicates of the latter were issued by the British Government, and new trustees appointed, by whom the fund—now amounting to nearly forty thousand pounds—is well and faithfully administered.

The front gate is a rich specimen of the florid Saracenic that characterises most of the neighbouring buildings, and two Sphynxes guard the entry. Passing under the main arch one comes upon a large quadrangle, with a long raised platform, at the end of which stands a statue of a cow suckling her calf. At the farther extremity stands the main hall, containing pier-glasses, chandeliers, *tazias*, and other glittering gewgaws. The floor is paved with highly-polished marble, and the roof beneath the dome is vaulted. On one side stands a white building understood to be intended as a copy of the Taj of Agra, the worst of the many attempts of the kind in different parts of India, as the Mausoleum of Safdar Jáng at Dehli is the best and largest.

Most of the buildings of this enclosure are in a style that is fantastic without being light; and the stucco is coloured in distemper in the glaring taste that spoils so many of the Lucknow edifices. But when the enclosure is illuminated for a festival it is bright and effective: and deserves notice as the only remaining complete specimen of the works of this kind which once characterised the metropolis of the province. One of these fêtes is stated to cost twelve thousand rupees a night.

From the Hosenabad it is but a short distance to the Gol Darwáza of the chauk, or narrow bazar already described, and close by is the Residence of a member of the late royal family, the Nawab Mohsin-ud-Daulah, famed for his persistent and well-tried loyalty to the paramount power.

On the other side is the *Júma Masjid*, or Cathedral Mosque, commenced by the last king out one, Amjad Ali, and completed, not long since, by a female of his family. It is a grand building, with the loftiest minarets in Lucknow, and a marble pavement. This fine edifice is well worth inspection.

MÚSAH BAGH.

We have now arrived at the last of the old garden houses of the late Rulers of Oudh, a noble site, comprising some eight acres of land enclosed in lofty walls with flanking defences. This was the last place held by the enemy, and they were driven out of it by a brilliant movement in Lord Clyde's attack of March 1858, of which it is now time to say a word.

LORD CLYDE'S ATTACK.

Of the three attacks made on Lucknow by the British, each adopted a different line. Havelock, advancing straight up the Cawnpore road, ran the gauntlet of all the front of the enemy's defences, from the *Húyát Buksh*, by the *Hazrot Gunj* up to the *Kaisar Bágh*. His loss was proportionably great. When Sir Colin Campbell advanced to relieve the joint forces of Havelock and

Inglis in the following November, he expected that the enemy would be prepared for him on that line; the wily Scot therefore went off to the right by way of the Martiniere; and though his loss was severe—43 officers and 450 men killed and wounded—yet, considering that they had turned an enemy of five times their strength out of a number of fortified positions, and that they effected their purpose of rescuing the whole of the women and children, destroying the guns, and bringing off the treasure, it may be admitted that the price was not too high to pay for what was obtained. On coming back a second time, Campbell—now raised to the peerage as Baron Clyde—suspected that the enemy would fall into their old mistake of looking for him upon the line of his last advance. He therefore resolved to disappoint them once more; and crossed the chief portion of his forces by a bridge of boats not far from the present Railway bridge by the *Dilkusha*. The event justified his forethought; for the enemy, as he had anticipated, had prepared to meet him on the old road, behind three strong lines, extending from the canal to the *Kaisar Bágh*. But it had never occurred to them that the attack would be conducted, this time, still further to the north ; and therefore they had neglected to build returning walls on the side of the river. The British accordingly protected by a good cavalry force under Sir Hope Grant, marched up the left bank of the Gumti ; and after successively enfilading the whole of the three defending lines, crossed over by the bridges, and took the enemy in rear. But for some misunderstanding, that was never cleared up, their retreat would have been cut off; as it was, the pursuit was too late to be of very much effect. This circumstance was much deplored at the time, though perhaps not so deservedly as if it had happened in a more foreign war, and where ultimate conciliation was not the object. It was stated at the time that the escape of the rebels was due to the excessive caution of Lord Clyde, and his friend Sir Hope Grant; in a book* published sixteen years later confirms the belief.

* Incidents of the Sepoy War, by Henry Knollys, 1873, p. 279.

CONCLUSION.

On the northern side of the river there are a few houses, of which the chief is known as *Díl Arám*, or 'Hearts' ease," and some garden enclosures; but they are of no interest, either architectural or historical. The Seraglios of the Nawabs; the annexation and its consequences; the defence and the pacification; these make up the story of Lucknow.

APPENDIX A.

The following account of the Government Flour Mills (reckoned to turn out 7 or 8 tons daily) was obtained too late to be inserted in the text of the present edition. The Mills rank deservedly among the industries of Cawnpore :—

Government Flour Mills, Cawnpore, were erected to supply a pure quality of flour to the Military Stations in the North-West.

They were completed, June 1869, and cost in erecting machinery and 5-storey building, condensing water tanks, and chimney 100 feet high, Rs. 37,000. This sum does not include the machinery which consists of three cornish boilers, one compound beam engine, seven pairs of French mill stones, five pairs worked by Bovell's Patent, *viz.*, passing a current of cold air through the stones while at work by means of a fan.

There is also another fan to take the hot air and dust into a small room in the fourth floor of the Mill. After the wheat is ground, it is passed by screws and elevators to the silk dressers. These consist of reals 28 feet long, 3 feet 6 inches diameter, covered with Swiss silk, varying from 4,900 to 8,100 meshes per square inch.

The whole of the work, as far as possible, is done by machinery. There are 42 natives of all grades employed. This includes boys and apprentices.

The consumption of wheat varies according to the demand for flour, sometimes as much as 9,000 maunds per month. The Mills are capable of manufacturing a steady out-turn of 20 maunds of flour per hour. The whole of the flour, bran, &c., produced, is consumed by Government: the flour for the troops, the bran for cattle and horses, the atta for elephants. The flour is all dispatched to the various stations by rail in 2-maund bags, except for hill stations, when $1\frac{1}{4}$-maund bags are used, as two bags make a mule load.

It is proposed that the Oude and Rohilcund Railway should lay a branch line from the new Station to the Mills. There are twenty stations supplied by the Mills besides outposts, *viz.*, from Umballa to Dinapore, and from Barielly to Jubbulpore.

APPENDIX B.

TOMBS WITHIN THE ASRAPORE ORPHANAGE COMPOUND.

Description of tombs.	Position or direction.	Epitaph.
Monument, brick masonry work, marble tombstone, with compound wall.	East	STUART BEATSON.
Brickwork, with stone slab placed flat. Sand tombstone standing at the head.	West	Sacred to the Memory of CAPTAIN EUGENE CURRIE, 84th Regiment, who was mortally wounded at the action of Cawnpore, and died on the 19th July 1857, in the 32nd year of his age.
Also		
Two mounds of Native Soldiers, one at the head, and another at foot.	Do.	No inscription.
Brickwork, convex shape marble tombstone, with wooden fence.	North	Sacred to the Memory of MAJOR S. G. C. RENAUD, of the 1st Madras Fusiliers, who died on the 21st July 1857 from the effects of a wound received in action against the rebels on the 15th July 1857.
Nine tombs, orphans	Do.	No inscription.

K

APPENDIX C.

Extract from the Treaty of A.D. 1801.

"ARTICLE I.

"His Excellency the Nabab Vizier hereby cedes to the Honorable the East India Company, in perpetual sovereignty, the undermentioned portions of his territorial possession, amounting in the gross revenue to one crore and thirty-five lakhs of rupees, including expenses of collection, in commutation of the subsidy, of the expenses attendant on the additional troops, and of the Benares and Furruckabad pensions.

Statement of the Jumma.

		Rs.	A.	P.
Chuckla Korah, Kurrah, and Chuckla Etawah		55,48,577	11	9
Kehr and others		5,33,374	0	6
Furruckabad and others		4,50,001	0	0
Khairaghur and others		2,10,001	0	0
Azimghur and others, Azimghur, Mownaut Bunjun ...		6,95,624	7	6
Goruckpore and others & Butwal.	Goruckpore, &c.... 5,09,853 8 Butwal 40,001 0	5,49,854	8	0
Soubah of Allahabad and others		9,34,963	1	3
Chuckla Bareilly, Asophabad & Kelpoory ...		43,13,457	11	3
Nababgunge, Kehly and others		1,19,242	12	0
Mohoul and others, with the exception of the Talook of Arwul		1,68,378	4	0
Total Jumma, Lucknow Sa. Rs. ...		1,35,23,474	8	3

ARTICLE 2.

"The subsidy which, by the second Article of the Treaty of 1798, His Excellency engaged to pay to the Company (now that territory is assigned in lieu thereof and of the expenses of the additional troops) is to cease for ever; and His Excellency is released from the obligation of defraying the expenses of any additional troops which at any time may be required for the protection of Oude and its dependencies, whether of the countries ceded to the Company or the territories which shall remain in the possession of His Excellency the Vizier.

ARTICLE 3.

"The Honorable the East India Company hereby engage to defend the territories which will remain to His Excellency the Vizier against all foreign and domestic enemies; provided always that it be in the power of the Company's Government to station the British troops in such part of His Excellency's dominions as shall appear to the said Government most expedient; and provided further that His Excellency retaining in his pay four battalions of infantry, one battalion of Nujeebs and Muwattees, two thousand horsemen, and to the number of 300 Golundauz, shall dismiss the remainder of his troops, excepting such numbers of armed peons as shall be deemed necessary for the purposes of the collections and a few horsemen and Nujeebs to attend the persons of the Aumils.

ARTICLE 5.

"That the true intent and meaning of the 1st, 2nd, 3rd and 4th Articles of the Treaty may be clearly understood, it is hereby declared that the territorial cession being in lieu of the subsidy, and of all expenses on account of the Company's defensive engagements with His Excellency, no demand whatever shall be made upon the treasury of His Excellency on account of expenses which the Honorable Company may incur by assembling forces to repel the attack or menaced attack of a foreign enemy,—on account of the detachment attached to His

Excellency's person—on account of troops which may occasionally be furnished for suppressing rebellions or disorders in His Excellency's territories—on account of any future change of military stations,—or on account of failures in the resources of the Ceded Districts, arising from unfavorable seasons, the calamities of war, or any other cause whatsoever."

Treaty of 1837.

"ARTICLE 1.

"Article third (3rd) of the Treaty, dated the tenth of November, one thousand eight hundred and one, is hereby cancelled and His Majesty the King of Oude may employ such a military establishment as he may deem necessary for the government of his dominions. His Majesty engages, however, to make a suitable reduction of his establishment, when it may appear to the British Government, from its pressure on the finances of the country or other causes, to be obviously excessive * *

* * *

ARTICLE 7.

"In modification of Article 6th of the Treaty above referred to, it is hereby provided that the King of Oude will take into his immediate and earnest consideration, in concert with the British Resident, the best means of remedying the existing defects in the police, and in the Judicial and Revenue Administrations of his dominions, and that if His Majesty should neglect to attend to the advice and counsel of the British Government or its local representative, and if (which God forbid) gross and systematic oppression, anarchy and misrule should hereafter at any time prevail within the Oude dominions, such as seriously to endanger the public tranquillity, the British Government reserves to itself the right of appointing its own officers to the management of whatsoever portions of the Oude territory, either to a small or to a great extent, in which such misrule as that above alluded to may have occurred, for so long a period as it may deem necessary, the surplus receipts in such case, after defraying all charges, to be paid into the King's treasury, and a true and faithful account rendered to His Majesty of the receipts and expenditure of the territories so assumed.

ARTICLE 8.

"And it is hereby further agreed that in case the Governor General of India in Council should be compelled to resort to the exercise of the authority vested in him by Article 7th of this Treaty he will endeavour, as far as possible, to maintain (with such improvements as they may admit of) the native institutions and forms of administration within the assumed territories, so as to facilitate the restoration of those territories to the sovereign of Oude when the proper period for such restoration shall arrive."

[These extracts are from *Aitchison's Treaties and Sunnuds*, Vol. II, where we are also informed that the non-approval (by the Court of Directors) of the Treaty of 1837 was ***never communicated*** to the Oude Government.]

APPENDIX D.

The following facts regarding the history of the Martiniere School are taken from the report of Mr. A. Lawrence, the Commissioner employed by the Government of India to inspect such institutions in 1871 :—

"A few years after the foundation of the Calcutta school, the Supreme Court, with the sanction of the Governor General, by an order dated 11th April 1839, appointed the Secretary to the Government in the General Department and the Government Agent for the time being Trustees for the Martin Charities at Lucknow, that effect might be given to the charitable bequests of the late Major-General C. Martin. The Trustees were requested to prepare a scheme for the management of the College and conformably with the provisions of the will, to the amount of the funds set apart for the purpose, and to the condition of the King of Oudh that the Christian religion is not to be taught except to those who voluntarily desire it.

"A long time elapsed, and a large sum of money, Rs. 2,69,107, was spent before the buildings were ready to receive pupils. The College was at last opened on the 1st October 1845 with a nominal register of 97 pupils. By March 1847, 132 were enrolled; one-fifth Christians, two-fifths Musalmans, and two-fifths Hindoos."

We are elsewhere told that 65 Christian boys only entered the Residency on the 18th June 1857. Of these, four were boarders and 61 foundationers; two of the former died during the siege, but among the latter there were no casualties, and only two were returned as wounded. The elder boys were armed and did military duty; others worked the telegraph, and a number were usefully employed in hospital in attending on the sick.

"After marching out with the relieving force, and after a short stay at Allahabad, the school reached Benares on the 15th January 1858, where it had been determined temporarily to locate it. During their residence at Benares the numbers were somewhat small, and but 68 (all Christians) returned to Lucknow on the 23rd March 1859.

"Four classes of students are entertained by the College.

"I. Foundationers.—These are entirely supported, clothed, and educated out of the funds of the institution. Their number is limited to eighty.

"II. Boarders.—The sons of parents who can afford to pay for them according to the scale laid down in Rule V. The number of boarders is at present limited to eighty.

"III. Day Scholars.—Boys whose parents reside at or near Lucknow, and who receive instruction only at the College.

"IV. Day Boarders.—These are the same as day scholars, except that in addition to their education they are provided with breakfast and dinner at the College (*vide* Rule 21).

"N. B.—In the College all classes are treated alike.

"The first mention of this class of boarder foundationers is in the proceedings of 1861. There had been boarders previous to, and after, the mutiny, and apparently at various rates of payments, but at this time a new term—boarder foundationers—was employed, and parents were invited to send children at Rs. 6 and Rs. 12 monthly. The scheme appears not to have answered, as since 1866-67 there is no mention of them. The schemes of 1870 and 1872 propose to receive this class, but at the expense of the free foundation. The Calcutta Martiniere is bound to keep up a certain number of free boys and girls. There seems to be no such condition extant at Lucknow, but it has been the practice to consider half the boarders free and half paying.

"Rules have been passed, but not kept to; and it is now impossible to ascertain anything with certainty.

"After the re-establishment of the College in 1859, things went on much as they had done before. The Principal certainly raised the tone of the College, and, by deporting the Native Department to the city of Lucknow, put the Martiniere in the way of becoming a great English school.

"Up to the year 1867 the avowed object of the school was to prepare a few boys for the Entrance Examination to the 1st Department, Roorki. Between 1863 and 1867, of the twenty-three students who passed out of the 1st Department, eight were educated at La Martiniere, Lucknow.

"In 1867 the College was affiliated to the Calcutta University; the course of education was to a certain extent diverted; but at Christmas, 1868, out of seven boys sent up, four passed in the 1st class, two in the 2nd, and one failed in Latin. In 1869 no boys went up. In 1870, of six candidates four were successful in gaining each a 1st class. Five candidates were sent up for the Entrance Examination of the Calcutta University, 1871, and all of them were successful, two boys being placed in the 1st class, and three in the 2nd."

As to the girls' school, it is added that "the children are divided into five classes in school, and their education is described as plain, practical, and religious.

"The subjects taught are—

"The Bible and Scripture History, Grammar, Reading, Writing, and Arithmetic.

"History, especially English and Indian, Geography, and General Knowledge.

"Map-drawing

"Plain and fancy needlework, knitting, house-keeping and household accounts.

"Music (as an extra) separately charged.

"Special classes may from time to time be formed, on the report of the head mistress, at the discretion of the committee."

INDEX.

Page.